PATHETIC FALLACY
IN THE
NINETEENTH CENTURY

PATHETIC FALLACY IN THE NINETEENTH CENTURY

A Study of a Changing Relation Between Object and Emotion

BY

JOSEPHINE MILES

1 9 6 5

OCTAGON BOOKS, INC.

NEW YORK

Originally published 1942, by University of California Press
New preface copyright© 1965 by Josephine Miles

Reprinted *1965*
by special arrangement with University of California Press

OCTAGON BOOKS, INC.
175 FIFTH AVENUE
NEW YORK, N. Y. 10010

LIBRARY OF CONGRESS CATALOG CARD NUMBER: 65-16786

Printed in U.S.A. by
NOBLE OFFSET PRINTERS, INC.
NEW YORK 3, N. Y.

PREFATORY NOTE

THIS STUDY follows one on "Wordsworth's Vocabulary of Emotion" (Univ. Calif. Publ. English, Vol. XII, No. 1) by centering upon a device within that vocabulary and by extending observation of the device through a century and more to show how its history represents a major change in thought.

The work has been made possible by the Fellowship Crusade National Fellowship of the American Association of University Women for 1939–1940, and by the steadfast kindness of Professor Benjamin H. Lehman and the Department of English of the University of California.   J. M.

PREFACE TO THE OCTAGON EDITION

Much as the attribution of human feeling to the natural world has been criticized, its absence in modern poetry may provide some basis for criticism too. Where has it gone, the feeling world? All into symbol? As the major poetic vocabulary of the present is mostly terms of natural objects—*wing, shadow, rain, stone, hill, grass*—and as there is no major modern vocabulary of feeling, the objects are unattached, or carry their significance by context. For example, the chief adjectives of Thom Gunn's first book are *dead* and *great,* the chief verbs, *come, feel, find, go, hold, keep, know, leave, lie, make, move, see, take, think, turn, want,* and these work upon chief nouns like *bird, body, bed, ground, head, street, wind* and *world*—a context for deepest emotion, but perhaps not for attribution of it. Gunn's "Human Condition" begins:

Now it is fog, I walk
Contained within my coat;
No castle more cut off
By reason of its moat:
Only the sentry's cough,
The mercenaries' talk.

The street lamps, visible,
Drop no light on the ground,
But press beams painfully
In a yard of fog around.
I am condemned to be
An individual.

> In the established border
> There balances a mere
> Pinpoint of consciousness.
> I stay, or start from, here:
> No fog makes more or less
> The neighbouring disorder.

So also the first two stanzas of "The Truth the Dead Know" in Anne Sexton's *All My Pretty Ones*:

> Gone, I say and walk from church,
> refusing the stiff procession to the grave,
> letting the dead ride alone in the hearse.
> It is June. I am tired of being brave.
>
> We drive to the Cape. I cultivate
> myself where the sun gutters from the sky,
> where the sea swings in like an iron gate
> and we touch. In another country people die.

Or the first lines of A. R. Ammons' "Risks and Possibilities" in *Expressions of Sea Level*:

> Here are some pretty things picked for you:
>
> 1)   dry thunder
>   rustling like water
>   down the sky's eaves
>
>   is summer locust
>   in dogfennel weed
>
> 2) the fieldwild
>   yellow daisy
>   focusing dawn
>
>   inaugurates
>   the cosmos
>
> 3) the universe comes
>   to bear
>   on a willow-slip and
>   you cannot unwind
>   a pebble
>   from its constellations

In all these versions of the natural world, things mean or be not in themselves but as objects which are under pressure from meanings beyond them. As symbols implying emotions often unstated or attitudes so complex as to be unstatable, they have taken the place of the more analytical "fallacy" in our poetry. Rather than relation, they emphasize either fusion or disrelation. The "pathetic" has taken on new meanings, in its move from simple attribution to complex implication.

JOSEPHINE MILES
December 1964

CONTENTS

I. INTRODUCTION

THE ATTRIBUTION of feeling to things, which Ruskin called pathetic fallacy, is more than a device mentioned in rhetoric books; it is a way of seeing the world and expressing the view. It is a selection and a stress of what its employer considers poetically significant. In the century before Ruskin, it was of prime importance to poetry and was used abundantly, with care and with consistency, by Gray, Collins, Beattie, Cowper, Burns, Blake, Darwin, Wordsworth, Scott, Byron, Shelley, Keats. In the century after Ruskin's derogation of it, its use and importance, for Tennyson, Browning, Rossetti, Morris, Swinburne, Hopkins, Meredith, Housman, was only one half, or less, as great as before. For T. S. Eliot, whose influence on current poetry makes him a possible modern representative, the power of the fallacy is close to none at all.

It is presumable, then, that since the device declined in so clearly traceable a line, changing its inner character in a fashion equally traceable, it must have been controlled by a combined force of thought and poetic convention which kept it from any large vagaries of individual will. It was, apparently, not just for the poet to choose whether he would use any of the device or no; the poet thought and saw within the margins of his time and took this basic phrasing as a matter of poetic course. That *mountains mourned,* that *winds sighed,* that *fields smiled,* that *trees were in a happy mood,* that, in other words, natural objects were given the feelings and powers of human estate, was a truth solid in poetry as a prime poetic substance. It was prime in poetry because it was prime in philosophical thought and in plain everyday vision; so one may assume from its consistent and vigorous use.

The questions then arise: first, To what theory of objects was the pathetic fallacy so intrinsic in the "Romantic" period? second, What was the major controlling and abiding change of thought in the 1840's, a period not usually marked as significant for vital change in poetry and language? and third, What is our own practice now, and what can we see in poetry through the eyes of the fallacy?

Part of the last question has a simple and important answer: our present attitude toward the pathetic fallacy is one of indifference or dislike, at least on the critical level. It is a trite device, representative of a past period. We don't use it; we just note it. We say,

Our mountains do not frown, our trees do not dance in the wind, our sunbeams do not smile. We struggle to avoid the pathetic fallacy and prefer the way of Peter Bell to that of his critic.[1]

We think, contrary to Peter Bell and Wordsworth his critic, both, that the yellowness of the primrose by the river's brim is pretty important in itself and that the flower is important in itself. In stressing these terms, the object *in itself, for itself, objectivity, exteriority,* we build up a structure of poetic values which ignores attribution of feeling and so finds no place for discussion of the pathetic fallacy in good modern criticism, making it familiar only in schoolbooks. By ignoring the thing we ignore a very primacy in the poetry we inherit, and by ignoring the course of its decline we misjudge the Victorians in their "romanticism." The current criticism and literary revaluation by Brooks, Ransom, Tate, Colum, Winters, Empson, Leavis is full of illuminating agreements in establishing a modern position. One of these agreements is that the poetic language of the nineteenth century was a vague, diffused, and too connotative falling-off from the vigors of the seventeenth century. Nineteenth-century poetry, they say, surrendered its hard core of meaning to science and itself retired to the thinning margins of suggestion.

---

[1] George Boas, *Philosophy and Poetry*, pp. 10–11. But D. G. James defends the fallacy as opposed to the idea of the "object in itself," in *Scepticism and Poetry*, pp. 85–87; and Allen Tate speaks of "the standard poetics of our own time—projection of feeling," in *Reason in Madness*, p. 58.

Observation of so small a device as Ruskin's condemned pathetic fallacy indicates, however, that Victorian language had more than a falling-off, it had a precise contribution of its own to make, and a contribution with which we are still today deeply concerned: the phrasing of sense perception through adjectives of temperature, texture, color, shape; and the phrasing of response to these with a lesser use of the standard terms of feeling. The poetry of such dramatic tensions as the seventeenth-century root metaphor represents had become the eighteenth-century poetry of associated object and emotion, and these standard "universal" associations had given way to a closer look at the object, a sight of its structure and proportion, and a consequent less stable definition of response, moving eventually into realms and problems of the unconscious.

Of these major motions of thought in the direction of sense qualities and their human significances the pathetic fallacy is a small and vivid representative. As it ceased to be a dominant factor in poetic expression (and by dominance I mean literal presence on every second page or so of a poet's work), it took to itself some of the new phrasing which was superseding it, and so contained in minute, but the more easily distinguishable, measure the elements of changing stress in thought and expression.

Yet the modern critics and historians of nineteenth-century poetry give us little notion of what to expect from its language, though language is often enlighteningly their focus. Their statements are general, and in terms of present aims and standards, without the assumption that present aims and standards have been established by the very explorations they call blurred. An alternative to the assumption that the centers of words stayed with science while their fringes went to poetry is the assumption that the centers of words themselves shifted as people looked for new central meanings. Since language is a tool adaptable to thought, rather than a fixed entity which thought assails at various points, it seems to me that the latter assumption is the more legitimate one.

What, then, were central meanings for the nineteenth century? The question has been answered in terms of large attitudes; I should prefer the means of small clues, which, so far, we have few of. The common answers, "penchant for Infinity," "materialism," "nature as hostile," "Hegelian idealism," indicate, at our distance, much less about poetry as it was written than the actual poetic materials indicate concerning the isms. Between the large attitudes and the individual contexts there is, in other words, a common realm of stress and agreement with respect to materials and perspectives, and it is this agreement which reveals itself most clearly in the conventions of poetry and establishes clear constants through the variables of individual practice.

So, though very little of importance has been said about the device of pathetic fallacy since Ruskin condemned it, the treatment of objects, in which it is involved, has undergone change and critical statement of change which are of greater importance. My problem of study, then, is one of minor and detailed observation. Little debate, argument, or adding up of signposts into proof is involved. There is no bibliography central to the material except the work of the poets themselves. Standard studies of individual poets or of the period give little inkling of what exact words and phrases the poets used. The immediate problem is one of reading, counting, classifying with respect to contexts, tracing and comparing as between poets, the one small device called pathetic fallacy.

The label's associations may well be looked into first. What has been its career, how has it been used? The term is Ruskin's. In the third volume of his *Modern Painters,* published in 1856, after stressing the importance of seeing a thing as it is and as it is to be— the facts of the thing—and after praising the modern objectivity and unselfishness of his time in its new "passion for inanimate objects," Ruskin wrote sternly against emotional attributions to nature of false appearances "unconnected with any real power or character in the object, and only imputed to it by us."[2] Such imputation, rising from human passion and false sympathy, is the pathetic fallacy.

The temperament which admits the pathetic fallacy, is, as I said above, that of a mind and body in some sort too weak to deal fully with what is before them or upon them; borne away, or over-clouded, or over-dazzled by emotion; and it is a more or less noble state, according to the force of the emotion which has induced it.[3]

The worst, said Ruskin, was such coldblooded phrasing as "raging waves" and so on, in what was still thought to be proper poetic convention.

This is not, nor could it for a moment be mistaken for, the language of passion. It is simple falsehood, uttered by hypocrisy; definite absurdity, rooted in affectation, and coldly asserted in the teeth of nature and fact.[4]

This diatribe established Ruskin's derogatory phrase in the language of criticism. Arnold and Morris defended the device partially; at least they explained what manner of enthusiasm had brought it into being.[5] E. S. Dallas in 1866 carefully associated it with the whole large division of poetic view which he called the egotistic or lyrical, and supported it, with perspective wider than ours now, as a kind, rather than a degree, of poetry.[6] Meredith took Ruskin's stand when he criticized some poetry of Stevenson on reeds which "you deprive of their beauty by overinforming them with your sensations."[7] Palgrave, the popular interpreter and preserver through the *Golden Treasury* of certain selected values, explained as "clothed in hues of human passion . . . what Mr. Ruskin may imply by 'the pathetic fallacy.'"[8] And Amy Lowell,

---

[2] *Modern Painters*, Vol. III, Pt. IV, chap. xii, §4.
[3] *Ibid.*, §8.
[4] *Ibid.*, §15.
[5] Lionel Trilling, *Matthew Arnold*, p. 91.
[6] Eneas Dallas, *The Gay Science*, pp. 273 ff.
[7] George Meredith, *Letters*, I, 290.
[8] Francis Palgrave, *Landscape in Poetry*, pp. 8–9.

speaker for the twentieth-century version of Imagism, stressing its exteriority, emphasized the fact that the thing was to be separated from personal response to it, and thus "unencumbered by the 'pathetic fallacy.'"[9]

The problem of relation between self and object, in other words, maintained its force throughout the century, using through all that time the terminology which Ruskin had established, and tending in more or less degree to his view that the bestowal of passion was an extra addition to, if not a distortion of, the significance of the object "in itself." On the other hand, in the hundred years *before* Ruskin's derogatory label, what had been important about the device was that its position was not such a secondary, but a primary one: the object had no significance in itself apart from the bestowal of, or explicit connection with, human passion. Wordsworth wrote: "All just and solid pleasure in material objects rests upon two pillars, God and Man."[10] And of his own "White Doe":

Throughout, objects ... derive their influence not from properties inherent in them, not from what they are actually in themselves, but from such as are bestowed upon them by the minds of those who are conversant with or affected by those objects. Thus the Poetry, if there be any in the work, proceeds whence it ought to do, from the soul of Man, communicating its creative energies to the images of the external world.[11]

Wordsworth thus provides a favorable term, *bestowal,* for some part of what Ruskin later was to call fallacy; and his whole philosophy of bestowal sets it up as basic truth, the reverse of fallacy.

[9] Amy Lowell, *Six French Poets,* p. 215.

[10] Wordsworth, *Early Letters,* ed. De Selincourt, p. 527.

[11] Wordsworth, *Letters: Middle Years,* ed. De Selincourt, II, 705. O. J. Campbell in *Wordsworth and Coleridge,* ed. Earl Leslie Griggs, explains this statement of Wordsworth's differently, as expressing a new kind of symbolism, opposed to Wordsworth's earlier naturalism. It seems to me, however, that Wordsworth consistently from the first stressed the idealizing effect of soul and imagination on object. See note to early "Evening Walk," in his Preface discussions of imagination, and, for sum, my *Wordsworth and the Vocabulary of Emotion.* James V. Logan, in "Wordsworth and the Pathetic Fallacy," *Mod. Lang. Notes,* LV (1940), 187–191, makes a close and interesting comparison between Wordsworth and Ruskin, but slights, I believe, the implications of such expression as this by Wordsworth.

Sir T. D. Lauder carried this view to the very borders of Ruskin's new world, expressing the attitude in his "Essay on the Origin of Taste" introducing his reprint of Uvedale Price in 1842, in what Mr. Ladd calls its fullest psychological development before the Victorian era.

> . . . the beauty which we impute to objects is nothing more than the reflection of our own inward emotions, and it is made up entirely of certain little portions of love, pity, and affection, which have been connected with these objects; and still adhere, as it were, to them, and move us anew whenever they are presented to our observation.[12]

In the 1840's and 1850's, then, the object both continued for many its old power of bestowed significance and increased for some the new power of "its own" significance, as the age looked more deeply into its nature and form. The Wordsworthian bestowal had its poetic acceptance, but Ruskin called it fallacious, and that label was accepted too.

The name-calling was done when the device named had already entered into its decline. While the old poetic position was well stated, the new poetic position had already been taken. It is this shift in its wider significance which is here to be observed in its detail.

The major problems of such study of detail are two: first, the problem of definition; second, the problem of representation. Since the method is experimental, the solutions are tentative, provisional upon their practical value as it is worked out by many more attempts than mine.

First, as to definition: since the "powers of human nature" which may be attributed to objects are so varied, I arbitrarily limit them here to the powers of emotion and passion, which are most central to the "pathetic." That is, I count as an instance of the pathetic fallacy every attribution of a named emotion to an object; and the regular signs of emotion, such as tears and laughter, are

---

[12] Henry Ladd, *The Victorian Morality of Art*, p. 93.

included.[13] Thus *the trees were gay, the mountains mourned, the proud fields laughed, the hills sadly slept* are all examples. If one emotion applies to two objects, or vice versa, it is counted as two instances. If ten instances are to be found in one hundred lines of a poem or poems, then the frequency of appearance is one in ten; this is the basis of measure. With this as basis, so that one's own impressions do not distort the report of actual usage, further discriminations can be made within the devices, with respect to kind of object, kind of emotion, and variety of combination in thought.

Second, as to representation: since the detail is so great, one must choose between covering ground intensively or extensively, between observing many kinds of device in one poet's total work, one device in a few totals, or one device in many representative works. This study covers two centuries through twenty-four works or groups of works, attempting a view of a trend. It assumes, therefore, for example, that a group of poems from *Men and Women* represent Browning for our purposes as fairly as the complete poems of Gray or Collins, less in amount, represent them. A study of Browning alone might reveal most illuminating variations between early work and late, but such would be of subordinate importance here. Further, it is a question whether such work as Beattie's and Housman's is as representative of the course of minor poetry in their time as I think it now to be. A great many poets must necessarily be further studied.

At any rate, I have chosen the two dozen poets in order to cover as wide yet central a range as possible, and I have chosen what is accepted as characteristic work, when all was too much, and I have taken from one to two thousand lines to be a fair minimum,

---

[13] I take the "names of emotion" in the simplest sense, the words traditionally listed, "love, hope, fear, and so forth," in the dictionaries of the eighteenth and nineteenth centuries, the *Encyclopaedia Britannica* of 1797, and the *New English Dictionary*. What I. A. Richards in *Practical Criticism* (New York, 1930), pp. 217–222, proposes concerning this vocabulary, that it include words of evaluation such as *beautiful,* raises an interesting problem, but should not be used directly for a study in historical terms, since the poets themselves did not make these further discriminations.

while for key poets like Tennyson I have examined much more. Evidence of versatility within a thousand lines usually suggests whether the range should be widened.

The quantitative results of the observation are summarized in the appended table (p. 295). The two central sections of the study are discursive: they trace the steps of change and continuity within the pathetic fallacy, and then the changing world views and attitudes toward objects as evident in the prose of the times. One who is impatient with such detail and pedestrianism had best read only the conclusion in the light of the numerical table, though in fact the developing phrases of fallacy one by one are themselves the life in the study. The gist of the study is relatively brief to state, since it is more to be remarked for its implications than for its complications.

Its implications are fundamentally these: that every poetic device participates in a large world of thought and a common view and, when objectively observed, is a strong clue to the whole; that poetry and all other arts possess observable and significant prime constants with traceable careers; and that the pathetic fallacy was for a while one of these constants the recognition of which suggests some modification of criticism in our time.

We turn, then, to the actual progress of phrasing within the material: the entrenched *raging sea* against which Ruskin himself was to rage; then the breathing sympathies of the Wordsworthian object; then the words by which Burns, Scott, Keats, Shelley suggested, however faintly, that a new estate for objects was due; and finally, after 1840, the growing particulars of that new estate. The progress is phrase by phrase, because phrase by phrase the thought of the nineteenth century established itself in form.

II. POETRY

THE STANDARD for bestowal of feeling upon natural objects was well agreed upon, in quantity and quality, by those poets called Pre-Romantic who made statement of such bestowal a sizable part of their poetics. In contrast to Johnson and Goldsmith, who used little or no bestowal, Gray, Collins, Beattie, Burns, Cowper, the new feelers for nature, agreed on the value of the device with a unanimity which produced it once in every forty or fifty lines. The agreement carried over to some kinds of detail within the statement. Let us see what these statements of nature's feeling sound like.

Gray's, and we may assume here that they participate in a firm literary tradition, are concerned with zephyrs, hills, flowers, the morn, the deep, the land, the day. To these the statements attribute pleasure, happiness, cheer, smiles, laughter, fury, sorrow, anger, mourning, so that the phrases *laughing flowers, angry deep,* a *smiling land,* the *cheerful day,* become familiar. Their spirit, even as the isolated words suggest, was not one of inward nerve or sensitivity, but of outward expression: how the scene looks with the smile on the face of the land, the anger of the deep. Certain visible aspects are assumed as signs: a sunny peaceful look as a smile, the sign of joy; darkness and cold of tempest, the sign of anger. The likeness between men and nature, then, is a likeness of visible aspect associated with emotion. "Mountains, ye mourn in vain," is mourning by deepening of shadow and by veiling the head in cloud. In Gray's poetic scene is the gleam of pageantry, the gleam of objects dressed in their sympathetic countenance.

Collins provides the summary of the attitude in his line on Fancy, "Drest by her Hand, the Woods and Vallies smile." This is Fancy's hand, the Miltonic poet's hand, which settles mountain and mead in their moods, with their appropriate signs of feeling. It is a Fancy mainly visual for both Gray and Collins, but sometimes to be heard, as in Gray's ecstatic or sorrowing *lyre* and Collins' *sad'ning wind*. It is a Fancy which fits not only mourning to cloud, but also cloud to mourning; to be poetic the forces of scene and theme are required to combine; and they combine in terms of the shows of emotion, that least common denominator.

Emotion can show upon the face of the land better, upon this level of interpretation, than upon the faces of birds and animals, which, one would say, were more apt to feel. Animals and birds are used therefore by Gray and Collins, and by Beattie, who is another of their kind, rather as signs than as beings of inward feeling. Beattie's cock is the *proud harbinger of day,* his linnet sings a *lay of love,* his turtle *mourns,* and his peacock screams *discordant horror,* while Collins' Lion moves *in his Rage.* But the two bestowals of feeling in all the work of these three poets closest to a sense of plain immediate feeling in the outer world are two concerning animals: Gray's on his favorite cat, "Her conscious tail her joy declar'd," and Collins' on "heart-smit heifers," and "every herd by sad experience knows." The cat, the kine, not ranked too strictly in the ranks of type and visible sign, are able to experience and express, though briefly, these responses of their own.

Now cat and kine are going to be significant if we are to concern ourselves with the progress of the pathetic fallacy, for they in their joy and sad experience represent a sympathy which poetry was just about to philosophize upon, and for which Burns's favorite tim'rous beastie was to be a notable spokesman. For though Burns and Cowper went straight on in the tradition of winter's *angry howl, smiling sky,* and *gay lark,* with minor additions of emotions to *Nature* and *Earth,* both had a new notion of the feelings of nature, and these feelings were, for both, to be found and spoken of poetically in the world of the heifer and the cat. It would be possible to say: this was experienced, rather than typical or representative, nature; the lark's song *stood for* gaiety, while the feeling of the heart-smit cow must come from looking familiarly in the cow's sad eye. But the distinction is not exactly this. Both treatments are representative in their way, both are generalized in spread. The lark-gaiety and lion-anger are representative of certain sights and sounds associated with certain emotions; the sad eye and joyful tail are representative of a relationship, a direct sympathizing and interpreting by man of beast, which was becoming philosophic and poetic material.

Part of Cowper's *Task* was to make plain as well as poetic this sympathetic attitude. In addition to his portion of laughing fruitful fields, in addition even to his scenes that were of a kind to permit of being introduced by such lines as *The spleen is seldom felt where Flora reigns,* he made a generalization:

> the love of Nature's work
> Is an ingredient in the compound man,
> Infus'd at the creation of the kind.

"The love of Nature's work," he indicates, particularly in the sixth book, includes a recognition of the feelings possessed by Nature's work in the form of Nature's creatures, and a sympathy with those feelings, and he attempts no distinction between the possible kinds of feelings of the various creatures—they all, man and beast and bird, in a simple way feel alike; therefore the sympathy need be the simplest recognition of common emotions going back to Eden, at loss of which place

> Ev'ry heart,
> Each animal of ev'ry name conceived
> A jealousy and an instinctive fear.

Now the sixth book of *The Task,* "The Winter Walk at Noon," is speaking particularly of the merits of more pleasant modern bonds of sympathy, its theme, "animals happy, a delightful sight," its *tim'rous hare,* its squirrel

> With all prettiness of feigned alarm,
> And anger insignificantly fierce,

speaking for the major point that it is a hard heart and dead to
love
> ... that is not pleas'd
> With sight of animals enjoying life,
> Nor feels their happiness augment his own.

This sober and careful consideration in blank verse was agreed
with in the very year of its publication by Burns's verses, which
put its principles into action in reverse, which called upon *spring,
sooty coots,* and *speckled teals* to mourn for Capt. Matthew Henderson in his "Elegy," which assured "Thee, Matthew, Nature's
sel shall mourn." The sympathy was now actively reciprocal.
Winter was called upon to respond:

> Thy gloom will soothe my cheerless soul,
> When Nature is all sad like me.

And in the "Humble Petition of Bruar Water" the water throughout the poem speaks in its own person for its own feelings. The
relationship with human beings has become more personal by
this year, 1785. Give and take of sympathy and emotional support are assumed, even if only as a device at times, between man
and beast, even between individual poet and beast, and, faintly
further, between man and general nature. Notably, too, the general nature, animal, and man are becoming less general in their
interassociation. When the speckled teal can be called upon to
mourn for Capt. Henderson, then bestowal of feeling is a poetic
force to be reckoned with, and the pathetic fallacy has come into
its own, in the extreme sympathy of its form.

We speak of extremes. The deep extremes of the pathetic bestowal were immediately to appear in Burns's time, both of them
in 1789, and both of them differing from Burns in vision of
natural feeling. These were the *Botanic Garden* of Erasmus Darwin and the *Songs of Innocence* (the *Songs of Experience* ap-
pearing five years later), of William Blake. One may be judged
tone deaf to consider them in any way together. Nevertheless,

they may illuminatingly be so considered, for both poetize a
world of nature by a vast metaphor—or symbol, as Blake would
have it—acting and feeling in human moods, bound by human
fears and tendernesses. In this poetry therefore, there is less of the
interaction of man and natural object (the mountain mourns for
man, or man feels the mournfulness of the mountain), and more
of the direct vision of one world in terms of certain phases of the
other, the phase of emotion here providing the core of the symbol.
What statement it establishes! Steel *loves* the pole to which it is
magnetized. The shine of metal is *gay*. Echo, the Alps, Etolia,
silence, rivers, branches, Toad, Mimosa, Thames, and China all
are passionate. These, Darwin's actors, are no longer representative of feeling-types, as were Gray's; they feel because they are
in the pictured World of the imagination, where there are no
limits to what can feel. Convention, in spite of Darwin's scientific
and poetic theory, limited a large part of his objects to smiling
groves and angry oceans in the tradition, but some amazing new
objects participated in his new world of feeling.

And Blake's new world? It was different, but it was as entire.
Its objects too were self-dependent—they sympathized by implication, by agreement of mood, but not by explicit mirroring.

> The moon, like a flower
> In heaven's high bower,
> With silent delight,
> Sits and smiles on the night.

Stream, hill, meadows, grasshopper, birds, all laugh in this
poetry, and it is laughter not to suit the scene or the sympathizer,
but from their own true pleasure as expressed in human terms.

The natural world is poetically expressible in human terms:
upon this Blake and Darwin were agreed. The consequence was
a poetry thicker with the pathetic bestowal than any here observed, a poetry using the device once every twenty or thirty
lines, as compared with the others' standard one in fifty. A device

so abundant as to appear on every single page amounts to a constant reference, an undercurrent, a theme of meaning; this is its structure in 1789: a basic metaphor in terms of emotion, by which man's world is superimposed upon the objective, and the two read together.

I stress the likeness of the two poets because their difference is so readily to be assumed: the one, the great mystic with an inward-looking eye and an immediate recognition of truth to be seen; the other, a ponderous scholar with a leaning toward outward obviousness, surface, and a bloating of fancy; the two, like Darwin's steel, must "love their poles." Blake draws the simple parallel, makes bird and child, himself and fly, alike in the sharing of emotion sent from God:

> And can He who smiles on all
> Hear the wren with sorrows small,
> Hear the small bird's grief and care,
> Hear the woes that infants bear—

> ... Then am I
> A happy fly.
> If I live,
> Or if I die.

> ... Look on the rising sun: there God does live,
> And gives His light, and gives His heat away,
> And flowers and trees and beasts and men receive
> Comfort in morning, joy in the noonday.

Not a single "fallacious" statement was made in the *Botanic Garden* with such simplicity and intensity. In contrast was the Darwinian sublime:

> —Roll on, YE STARS, exult in youthful prime,
> Mark with bright curves the printless steps of Time.

In the Darwinian world the shared emotions were, partially, workable as if mechanisms; in Blake's they were infused like sunshine.

Yet the pathetic fallacy, as it was given form by these two in special self-dependence and abundance, reveals some doubly strengthened characteristics. First of all, apart from its excursions into steel, oxygen, and foreign parts, it remained steadfastly centered on certain objects: for Darwin, birds, fields, leaves, rocks, waters, earth; for Blake, birds, woods, groves, flocks, vales, and streams. These we have found in all the other poets, and here as elsewhere they receive a direct attribution of feeling. The total effect of poetic context would mislead us if it were to suggest that the main body of bestowal in Blake and Darwin was not determined by the standard substance of the time. Further, there are interesting small likenesses to be noted. We have again in Blake the lion of pathetic tradition, in all his expectations of *Rage* and his sublimity, though here

> ... the lion's ruddy eyes
> Shall flow with tears of gold:

and the lion announces that Wrath has been driven away. The *Botanic* lion is merely *indignant*. We have in both poets the forms that rise from visualizing minds, the mind which saw pictures as necessary to poetry, the mind which saw a host of angels in the sun. We have the feeling animals of Burns and Cowper: the tender heart of Darwin's mother-bird, and the merry sparrow, the rejoicing lamb of Blake. Newest in detail, and it is a detail which both poets present, is the counting of flowers in the feeling realm. The *tim'rous floret's golden bell,* the physiology of the "sensitive plant," was the theme of the second part of Darwin's poem, and it was an extension for which phrases in Blake speak also, not merely in Augustan conventions such as his jealous rose, but in such simplicities as *a happy blossom* and the generalization that *flowers and trees and beasts and men receive* joy in the noonday. This is an important company, not merely for its assortment here, but for what it portends. The feelings are to be apprehended so delicately that they may be sensed in the motion of leaves and petals, not of necessity read abroad on the wide face of the mountainous meadowy scene.

In the full career of the pathetic fallacy, then, in this high time of 1789, the device just comes to touch upon the flower in its feeling form. The numerous proud roses, sighing lilies, and vegetable loves of Darwin's work do not have this feeling form; they are part of the picturing and personifying tradition. Yet his mimosa, *weak with nice sense* and trembling in the shade, his "sensitive plant," as he notes it, participates with Blake's *flowers and trees and beasts and men* in a physical consciousness of a universally infused emotion, an emotion more roughly felt but already tenderly sympathized with in cat, cattle, and field mouse of the time.

This is the edge of discrimination reached by the pathetic in the years before Wordsworth: the sense of emotion as physically felt within flower, beast, tree, depending on some universal source, not on man's pictorial imagination or his sympathy. But it must be remembered how far from this edge was still the more abundant expression, in the central and traditional form (for the late eighteenth century, apparently), of the visually representative scene: *the angry ocean, mourning mountains, smiling fields*. It is possible to recognize, through the device, the purpose behind it, its plan of the world. One of the key words was *physiognomy*. Significant emotions were as seen or heard expressed in typical form, not as individually physically felt. As Garrick, showing only his head between the curtains of the stage, could run in rapid change of expression, from placid smile to open-mouthed horror, the gamut of emotions as LeBrun had prescribed them, so the natural world as it lay open to view, typically in the ways the painters painted it, could likewise exhibit with the aid of sun and shadow the signs of serenity, solemnity, or storm, of pleasure or of wrath. Hills, vales, groves, rocks, streams, seas, all so large in size as to suggest large general rather than special personal emotions, could afford, in their formality, not only to express, but to express suitably, according to the needs of the poet's mood. Thence the move from decoration to sympathetic reciprocation of feeling was an obvious one, the feeling moving inward, away from visible or audible representation, by just the degree of sympathy indicated. I stress this visual and audible feeling type in nature because of its surviving force. It was major for Pope; it provided the main body of pathetic statement for all the poets we have been observing here. The joyful *scene* is the standard fallacy: general, representative, visible with standard expression, and participating often in some amount of sympathy. If this is the first standard to be established, and a closely conventionalized neoclassic standard it seems to be, it is surprising not only that it seems so natural to all the poets we have observed, but also, further, that it should be highly characteristic of Wordsworth's poetry, amounting to at least a quarter of his uses of the attribution of feeling. It was so strong a poetic element, this *scene,* with its *hills* and *vales,* that one may establish the hypothesis that to it Ruskin's complaint was most forcefully directed.

We have been concerned, however, with another element of importance also: the increasing particularity and physical sensitivity of live things. The things which are symbols for passions, the lion for rage, the lark for joy, the lamb and linnet for an innocent merriment, the fly, even, for his small intensity, persist from Pope through all the poets we have noted, even to Blake with his odd and excessive uses of them. Then, from another point of view, other miscellaneous animals and objects have participated in the poetic convention, from a sense of the playful familiar, a pleasure of classic poetry, which allowed to cats, bees, domestic utensils, Darwin's steel and oxygen, what you will, a system of human feeling for the humorous nonce. For Cowper and for Burns some of these two varieties of feeling creatures came together, the familiar miscellaneous untypical beasties were viewed at times in their feeling states, in their private lives, in all seriousness; and there, along with the inclusion of flowers in the feeling world, is perhaps the most important new version of the fallacy we have come upon. The versions of Darwin and of Blake are, on the whole, a separate problem. They both use the device excessively, relative to the standard as we have noted it, because each of them founds an all-inclusive system upon it implicitly. By artifice or by mystic vision, in their worlds *everything* feels; they use the device not as bestowal by man on nature, but as activity in a different realm. Meanwhile it is the animal which seems to feel for itself and to have emotions that the poet understands and shares, and the flower conscious of what it feels, and Bruar Water speaking for itself, that seem to indicate what new aspects poetry is about to use along with the *scene* for its vision of the outer world. It is certain, at least, that Cowper's theorizing on the importance of animals' happiness to the viewer is a kind of theorizing which will find welcome development in Wordsworth, the accepted authority in this business.

Along with Wordsworth as center, most of these poets—Blake and Burns especially, and later Byron, Shelley, Keats—wrote in a fashion which seemed of the utmost significance to one or another of the poets of Ruskin's time. Theirs are the names recurring in the letters, the journals, and the reported debates. Theirs are the poems the likeness of which in poetic substance to some Victorian attempts we wonder at and recognize. Into the work of Wordsworth, Byron, Shelley, Keats, then, we must look to see what became of the pathetic standard after its intense establishment, and what forms it may have taken that were later unacceptable to poetry.

Wordsworth provided a settling down, modification, and unification for the common terms. As has been noted here, a quarter of his uses were of the *scene* type of the past. His streams smiled, his leaves danced in glee, his dells and plains were happy, his groves cheerful. Further, he included most of the type animals, even in the *Lyrical Ballads:* the lark, the merry birds, the bee, the fly, the prancing steed, the lamb and lion. But too, like Burns, he was more specific, with reference to throstle and blackbird, and in three or four poems had Waterfall and Eglantine, Oak and Broom, speak like Bruar Water for themselves, of their own anger, grief, and joy. Wordsworth had, beyond these minor particularities and familiarities, a power of theorizing about the sympathetic relationship which gave it dimension. The relationship which Cowper had said a few words for, which Blake and Burns had tended to assume, Wordsworth wished to talk about directly and repeatedly. That infusing power which man, tree, beast, and flower felt alike and which provided the bond of sympathy between them, was, he was careful to assure himself, the power of feeling such emotions as love and hope and fear.

> . . . in that green bower
> The periwinkle trails its wreaths,
> And 't is my faith that every flower
> Enjoys the air it breathes.
>
> The birds around me hopped and played,
> Their thoughts I cannot measure,
> But the least motion that they made
> It seemed a thrill of pleasure.

It is not that they are suiting themselves to man's mood entirely; it is that they have their own.

> There is a blessing in the air,
> Which seems a sense of joy to yield
> To the bare trees, and mountains bare,
> And grass in the green field.

This is a quatrain close indeed to Blake's on God's light and heat and joy, however firmly the general and diffused contrasts to Blake's homely and familiar.

And Wordsworth, like Cowper, has a moral to establish. His "Hart-Leap" is the primer of ethics, the textbook of pathetic lore toward which the poets had been tending. The hart, being hunted, feels the emotions of a soul pursued, pride, fear, anger— a magnificence of emotion, in fact, which places him not among the lowly but among the noble. "His death was mourned by sympathy divine"—by that Being who is in the clouds and air and leaves, and who cares for those he loves. And the death teaches us by its consequences, by the lonely and unhappy spirit of the place of it,

> Never to blend our pleasure or our pride
> With sorrow of the meanest thing that feels.

We are not only to learn from the happiness of Cowper's animals, then; we are to suffer from the pain they suffer, and the spirit of the emotion is to be present in the surrounding atmosphere.

This explicit philosophy of the tender spread, and the mutual interdependence of feelings established for Wordsworth two special styles of pathetic statement in addition to the standard. One was a frequent use of what possibly should be called an inverted simile; actually it bespeaks the strength and ingrain of the transference tradition. Instead of having natural objects borrow feeling from men, men by simile feel in the manner of natural objects. The old dame is *gay* as a *linnet;* and of others: *happy as a wave; Not blither is the mountain roe; No dolphin ever was so gay/ Upon the tropic sea; As cheerful as a grove in Spring; as happy as the day.* These phrasings suggest how deep was Wordsworth's habit of thinking of natural objects in terms of their emotions. If we were to say *characteristic* emotions, and so we must in a measure, we should be indicating the extension of the type mode in this simile form. Such an extension Wordsworth does make: his roe and dolphin are chosen for visible characteristics of theirs which suggest certain visible signs of emotion in the traditional manner. But his use of this device of comparison is also evidently a part of his general idea that nothing is so full of the simple, primary, and pure emotions (and therefore the emotions best referred to) as the outer world of nature.

The second major phrasing deriving from this attitude is part of Wordsworth's finest and most characteristic method of expression, his delicate statement of just the infusing power of feeling which is central to his philosophy. The air is the bearer of the emotion, the breath of it; and by such metaphor as a matter of course the pathetic fallacy acquires a valuable amount of thinning out into spirit. The blessing of joy in the air, the *Such an entire contentment in the air, the voice of common pleasure,* speaking for the rivulet and the place's atmosphere, are phrases which add a new tone to the device of the pathetic. The spread to the air is a spread, also, to the sky: *both earth and sky/Keep jubilee,* and *The stars had feelings, which they sent/Into those favoured bowers.* These are a few phrases to be listed, a handful among the many of convention which Wordsworth used with apparent satisfaction. By their scarcity they suggest how slow the poetic vision was to change along any one line of sight, but by their presence they suggest the possibilities and directions of change, and illustrate in minute detail what has often been generalized upon by writers on the Wordsworthian style.

Wordsworth, as a major poet of nature, did not contribute in amount or in kind to the poetic body of the pathetic fallacy. Both the emotions he named and the objects he applied them to were part of a standard long set. His contributions were his poetic skill in generalizing upon the accepted theme and device, and his poetic sensitivity to the shading and fusing spirit possible to the theme and device.

Byron and Scott, the two great popular Romantics, used the pathetic bestowal as if it were an old shoe, comfortable but not highly important. Because of their great influence in the youthful reading of their Pre-Raphaelite followers, this attitude is noteworthy. Scott, in his "Lay of the Last Minstrel," made attribution of feeling to nature just half as often as Wordsworth, a fourth as often as Blake or Darwin at their mildest. Byron ranks with Scott, for though his "Childe Harold" is near to the standard in its usage, "Don Juan" falls far below. *Glad* winds, *pride* of Sierra and Sevilla, and the *angry tail* of the bull—these are Byron's eighteenth-century attributions. His most notable phrase is that *sunless shrubs must weep,* a wording of his own which suggests that though his main course was conventional in these terms, there may be other isolated individual bestowals in his work. Scott, too, emphasizes place names and *pride,* an Augustan emotion which was tending to disappear from its high place in poetry. *Sad scene, angry dog, smiling summer,* are all his kind, and handled without distinction. Scott's distinction comes in the new generalization he makes: he has an explanation of that by now well-known device, as yet unnamed pathetic fallacy. He clears the matter up for the layman, as if clarification were long overdue.

> Call it not vain:—they do not err,
>   Who say, that, when the poet dies,
> Mute Nature mourns her worshipper,
>   And celebrates his obsequies;
> Who say, tall cliff, and cavern lone,
> For the departed bard make moan,
> That mountains weep in crystal rill;
> That flowers in tears of balm distil;
> Through his loved groves that breezes sigh,
> And oaks, in deeper groans, reply;
> And rivers teach their rushing wave
> To murmur dirges round his grave.
>
> II.
>
> Not that, in sooth, o'er mortal urn
> These things inanimate can mourn;
> But that the stream, the wood, the gale,
> Is vocal with the plaintive wail
> Of those, who, else forgotten long,
> Lived in the poet's faithful song,
> And, with the poet's parting breath,
> Whose memory feels a second death.

The maiden of the poem shakes the tear from the rose, the chief groans and his tears become the stream. The created characters mourn in the created landscape, and the pathetic fallacy is clearly achieved with mirrors.

Scott, both in such an attitude as this and by his less frequent use of it, established the literary possibility of a new convention: the toleration of an artful device. Scott's emphasis was on the creating power of the poet, not the creating power of nature, as these were concerned with the sympathies of emotion. He had a story to tell; its characters lived so vividly in association with the landscape that landscape and characters shared emotion by the association; tree and stream sighed and wept, not out of feelings shared from above, but out of the artistry of the storyteller. This was, in a measure, a demotion for the fallacy philosophically; and, as it worked out, practically also, for the effect was to be gained less by a large pervasiveness than by a reminding touch of the device now and then.

This was the technique employed by the poet who was to be the favorite of the Pre-Raphaelites as children, the great youthful poet of the nineteenth century. This was the technique which Wordsworth expressly did not approve.[1] Perhaps before the century was half over it would have some positive effect toward change.

Meanwhile, both Keats and Shelley were, with apparent faithfulness to tradition, maintaining the abundance and the gusto of the pathetic fallacy in the early decades of the century. It is considered wiser now to view the differences of these two poets more particularly than their resemblances, but in respect to the pathetic fallacy some exception must be made. Obviously they agree on the importance of the device; they used it once every forty or fifty lines, as did most of their predecessors whom we have surveyed. They agree, too, in the exact conventional phrasing of many of their uses—though not, of course in the wider contexts

---

[1] See notes 6 and 7 below.

of these uses. It is for the moment surprising to see in these young writers of new intent so solid a structure of old poetic phrasing; the vivid detail of new growing out of old is brought to mind and made plainer in the small scope of the bestowal diction.

Here is the long-built-up vitality of *mournful waters, sad Echo, proud steed, happy hour, cliff* towering *proudly, sighing lily and rose* as emblems of hapless lovers, the *happy fields, glad day, nightingale's ecstasy, weeping cloud, And all the gloom and sorrow of the place.* These belong to Keats. And Shelley's flowers *weep,* whirlpools *race,* Moon *smiles,* he too has *sad Hour, amorous Deep, ocean's wrath, rejoicing sun;* and *Spring, nightingale, winds, ocean, thunder, Echo, mourning* for Adonais. Of the two, Keats seems a little the more closely bound to the convention. He employs even a smiling *Phoebus* and *Cynthia,* a *timorous brook,* and much *pride.* His fondness for the Spenserian and the Miltonic may have fostered the style, if it is from these that the force of the eighteenth-century fallacy gathered in English. At any rate, the set of feeling objects, the sympathetic pageantry of the scene, as established in Gray and Collins, is here maintained by Keats and Shelley almost a century later, as it has been maintained by Beattie, Cowper, Burns, Darwin, Blake, Wordsworth, Scott, Byron in the intervening years. Such is the strength of a poetic phrasing enforced by a view of the world.

Now secondly, what about the feeling animals which had arrived out of mere typed lion-rage and lark-gaiety, at so pretty a pass in the poetry of Wordsworth and Burns? They have somewhat subsided. Many are again types, such as Keats's *proud steed,* and *tiger-passioned, lion-thoughted* metaphor, and perhaps Shelley's *nightingale, eagle,* and *ring-dove's love-lament,* and those called upon to join in the lament for Adonais. Some few, though types, are as finely said as Keats's

> Nor let the beetle nor the death-moth be
> Your mournful Psyche, nor the downy owl
> A partner in your sorrow's mysteries.

This is straight representative association out of the eighteenth century, needing no further poetizing; yet the further poetizing it here shows itself capable of is remarkable at so full a stage of its maturity. But, as for the sensitive beasties who felt their own joys and fears, the animal happiness which Cowper recommended watching, these are scant in poets who attend to a richer kind of sensuousness and less of a direct sympathizing. Closest are Keats's *gnats* which wail in mournful choir, and minnows—*How they ever wrestle/With their own sweet delight,* and Shelley's birds with eyes *Bright in the lustre of their own fond joy,* and especially his   I have heard

> By mine own heart this joyous truth averred:
> The spirit of the worm beneath the sod
> In love and worship, blends itself with God.

These gnats, minnows, worms, however, for all the distinction of their passion as here expressed, are not of the "friends of man" variety; they represent the turn away from the memorable sympathy for the sad-eyed heifers to a more vivid physical attribution of feeling.

Such attribution, as it was delicately Wordsworth's, is also and more strongly these poets' gift to the pathetic fallacy. The feelings are translations of, conclusions from, felt and pervasive qualities, sensed by the touch and the hearing more than the sight. It has been noted that the poets with this sensibility made their bestowals often upon flowers, where the bond of feeling could not be direct but must be through fragrance and the motion and texture of petals. Such was the feeling of Keats and Shelley, in *A rose, convuls'd as though it smarted/With over pleasure*—and *a light of laughing flowers along the grass is spreading,* the flowers which sent *Their odorous sighs up to the smiling air.* Thence, though, is a divergence in the flower world. Shelley worked in a realm as particular, as scientific, as detailed, at once as mechanical and sympathetic as the garden wherein grew his "Sensitive

Plant." He crowned the whole course of the fallacy of feeling flowers with this long poem on the very subject. It was a Leviathan of a fallacy, next only to Darwin's, and a refinement of his. Keats, on the other hand, took no steps farther into the realm of what could be learned and said of flower feelings. His references sometimes were strictly classical, that is, in conformity with the standard of precedent: buds felt pride, rose was emblem, and a flower looking at its sad image did so for the sake of the story of Narcissus.

In this difference between a rich retention of convention and a violent expanding of it is a major difference between Keats and Shelley which the use of the one device reveals. But as a whole, the two develop the device as it were together, for both work with the thought of physical feeling strong in mind, and both spread to skies and shores as to flowers the sense of touch, temperature, and quality to go with feeling. *Deep in the shady sadness of a vale; the early sobbing of the morn;* the lyre to address a star *And make its silvery splendour pant with bliss;* and *All the sad spaces of oblivion:* all these connect the sensed qualities of object with its attributed emotion—shady with sad, silvery with bliss, sobbing with early, space with sadness. These are from Keats, and Shelley's: *a wide and melancholy waste/Of putrid marshes; the cold day/Trembled for pity of my strife and pain; that star's smile, whose light is like the scent/Of a jonquil when evening breezes fan it;* and the shore under the kisses of the sea, which

> Trembles and sparkles as with ecstasy,—
> Possessing and possessed of all that is
> Within that calm circumference of bliss.

All these phrases of an old bestowal sound enriched; it is the substance of color and shape which enriches them, and at the same time a suggestion of space or of waves which widen out into less of substance. So both poets, for example, attribute emotion to silence even: *the very sigh that silence heaves; and/Silence, too enamoured of that voice.* It is to be seen that the realm of emotional application is widening in two major ways: into more and more sensed detail, and into a wider universe of possibilities, the linking terms for the narrow and the vast being adjectives such as *sweet, silver, cold, calm,* the adjectives of touch and taste as well as sight and sound.

The special Romantic version of the fallacy, then, was one firmly up to the standard as we have seen it established, a standard of repeated emotions, repeated objects, and consequently recurring phrases, creating the half-pageantry of the imaged scene. It slighted only the sympathy phase of the standard, the Cowper-Burns-Wordsworth phase. It stressed with special delight the element strongly added by Wordsworth: the suggestion of the feeling in delicate and distant objects, the more vividly as the more tenuously sensed. And to this standard the young Romantic fallacy added its own vaster eye and its adjectival vigor.

Shelley's treatment of Wordsworth in "Peter Bell the Third" demonstrates his understanding of the Wordsworthian contribution of sensitivity. The feminine Nature who laughed as he touched her hem was not Wordsworth's or Peter's, she was more Burns's, as Shelley says. Wordsworth's were the songs of moor, glen, rocky lake, sky, earth, pedlars, parsons, and the mystery beyond these.

Thus—though unimaginative—
An apprehension clear, intense,
Of his mind's work, had made alive
The things it wrought on, I believe
Wakening a sort of thought in sense.

These so familiar lines state exactly the recognition of the nature of bestowal as it was being fostered in the early nineteenth century. In the midst of standard attributions these glimmerings are few, as in the few lines we have noted, but their presence at all is significant. "Thought in sense" as it wakens looks not at the face of nature, and not at the sympathetic feelings of its animals, but thinks by touch and feel, and reaches out beyond standard associations to the possible feelings of nature without a face but with an inner being of space and silence.

Three small evidences of the attitude of Keats and Shelley are these: first, that the world feels apart from man, as in Keats's shore—*Full of calm joy it was, as I of grief;* second, that Shelley adopts something of Scott's sense of the creative power of the artist in the voice of the fallacy, as in "Adonais," *His voice is one with Nature's;* and third, that in their lists of feeling natural objects the two poets make new inclusions: not only groves, rocks, hills, streams, not only Blake's beast and flower, but

> All he had loved and moulded into thought,
> From shape, and hue, and odour, and sweet sound,
> Lamented Adonais.

Shape, hue, odour, and sweet sound, these are the new agents of feeling, as the senses have acquired new powers. They spread away from *scene* into *air: Earth, ocean, air, beloved brotherhood!* They make more metaphysical even the standard Earth and Ocean as they dream

> Of waves, flowers, clouds, woods, rocks, and all that we
> Read in their smiles, and call reality.

Flowers and clouds, these are the objects of feeling in new detail, the one in small and "faint," the other in vast and vague. Here, as exactly as could be wished, one sees the change from eighteenth-century painting to nineteenth-century music take place in the mere combination of some few objects and adjectives. If, that is, *music*—as Mr. Babbitt has suggested[2]—is the term to be used. Rather, or at least, the change was one within, not of, a major world view: from the solids of a scene and the liquids of lark and stream to the vapors of cloud and airy fragrances. The changes are as slight and faint as their metaphors, but their presence as mist over the main body of the standard fallacy is significant.

---

[2] The major thesis of Irving Babbitt's *The New Laokoon.*

Meantime, at the end of this its century of prosperity the standard fallacy was solidifying in poetry, and solidifying poetry itself.
What inner current of excitement Keats and Shelley gave it
seemed as yet false. What inner current of excitement Wordsworth
had first felt in it was accepted for the sake of the larger philosophical interpretation and glow he put upon it. Cowper's advice
to sympathize with the happy animals, Burns's tenderness toward
the daisy, Wordsworth's own gradually accepted connections
between birds, flowers, and the human heart now were becoming
part of the realm of the nicest young ladies' attention, and so must
already have firmly established themselves in the world view of
the century. In the decades after Keats and Shelley it was Wordsworth who was taken to heart as never before—or after.[3] Just as
the major poetic material of the fallacy showed signs of the sea-
change, its widest audience recognized its traditional worth, and,
through the work of the flourishing minor poets under the shade
of Wordsworth, adopted the diction and the way of thought
which the standard prescribed. The new Annuals carried the
feeling flower into reading homes, and provided illustrations
also, so that even the little girls might learn to share the spiritual
sympathies along their garden paths. If *he* is blind to beautiful
landscape, suggested Praed's "Letter of Advice" in 1828,

> If he dotes not on desolate towers,
>   If he likes not to hear the blast blow,
> If he knows not the language of flowers,
>   My own Araminta, say "No!"[4]

It was the very sign of breeding that one should accept, half as
artifice and jest, half in serious and religious earnest, the fallacy
of happy streams and weeping winds.

A few years later, Thackeray was to write "A Word on the
Annuals" harder on them than they deserved, but indicating, as

---

[3] As Matthew Arnold said in his Preface to his edition of Wordsworth's poems, 1879.
[4] Quoted by Frederick E. Pierce, *Currents and Eddies in the English Romantic Generation*, p. 263.

we may note with glee, the very standard of the pathetic fallacy which the poets of the century since 1740 (at least) had been busy establishing. During the poetically dull decade and a half before 1840, while Jeffrey was bemoaning the state of writing and Wordsworth was coming into his most literal own, this was the pleasure, art, and virtue of the reader: *the scene.*

Miss Landon, Miss Mitford, or my lady Blessington, writes a song upon the opposite page, about a water-lily, stilly, shivering beside a streamlet, plighted, blighted, love benighted, falsehood sharper than a gimlet, lost affection, recollection, cut connexion, tears in torrents, true-love token, spoken, broken, sighing, dying, girl of Florence, and so on. The poetry is quite worthy of the picture, and a little sham sentiment is employed to illustrate a little sham art.[5]

Sham or no—and I think no, for the general reader was just beginning to feel himself capable of entering wholeheartedly into the spirit of an art the formal prime of which necessarily preceded its popular prime,—the old sentiment flourished while new creations languished. The 'twenties and 'thirties were a period of satisfaction: how well poetry expressed the spirit of God in nature and in man: love, romance, religion, what you will, breathed from breeze and tree, because, as Cowper had said, "God made the country and man made the town," and what God made was pure, beautiful, and representative of good. This blend of the major phases of fallacy which we have noted, the expressive face of Nature and its sympathetic breath, brings the device to its popularly consolidated position in the mid-century. The form of poetic phrasing and the form of general thought, so long interacting, now have reached such a degree of spoken familiarity that they are as quick to tongue as to feeling. Therefore for the leaders they are too easy, and they are ready for the ridicule of Thackeray, the shadings by poets of sensibility not yet recognized, and the childhood ponderings of the new generation of art.

---

[5] Quoted by Bradford Allen Booth, *A Cabinet of Gems,* Introduction, p. 15.

Until 1842 the youthful work of Tennyson had been ignored; in 1850 he was poet laureate. His was a poetry, once recognized, that went straight to the heart of acceptance, and it was the poetry, at first, of his early years, reordered and supplemented in the volumes of 1842. That was the material, the very material written in the reign of Wordsworth and the Annuals and recognizably colored by that unrecognized poet Keats, that hit the heart. What did Tennyson provide which the 1840's required so immediately? In respect to the pathetic fallacy, one would surmise: more of the same.

But actually, Tennyson, contrary to my expectation at least, used the device far less than the established standard of fifty lines to a bestowal. His frequency was about one in ninety lines. His thought regarding natural objects, still deeply full of qualities, scenes, and parallels as before, nevertheless concerned itself with a fundamentally different structure of relationship between nature and man. We are used, in the history of English poetry, to the pointing out of major breaks in concept and turning points of thought. As for the view of nature, Wordsworth is noted as such a turning point. But here, in small, in the specific field of a single device as it presents a major point of view, we find a different pattern of progression. Here Scott's was the rebellion against abundance and fervor, and Tennyson's was the offering of a new position, based on a strong, but more sparing, new variety of statement. His particular combination of convention and innovation needs exact looking into.

The following lines are characteristic of the new writing: they have qualities that were visible in Keats and Shelley and that are here outstanding.

> The broken sheds looked sad and strange . . .
>
> the brook that loves
> To purl o'er matted cress . . .
>
> . . . beating hearts of salient springs . . .

> Poor Fancy sadder than a single star,
> That sets at twilight in a land of reeds...

> All things that are forked, and horned, and soft
> Would lean out from the hollow sphere of the sea,
> All looking down for the love of me.

> ...the amorous odorous wind...

> The skies stoop down in their desire...

> The tearful glimmer of the languid dawn...

In these poems, the poems of youth and those included in the "Lady of Shalott" volume, winning the heart of the 'forties, for the first time the pathetic fallacy consistently expresses a new vision of things. The vision is one of sensed qualities, not objects, as the associates of human emotions. Immediately felt color and atmosphere takes the place of representative objects and arrangements. The adjective rather than the noun is clue to the emotion.

We have seen how angry storm or sea, smiling field, happy lark established themselves as standards. Basic to their significance was a concept of "essential" or "representative" quality, a single major quality, and the correspondence of this to the essential quality of the expressed form of an emotion. Darkening of the brow, tumultuous words, went with human wrath, as dark and tumult went with stormy sea; the storm could therefore be said to express the human feeling, and most directly and meaningfully by a kind of sympathy as metaphor for outward likeness. The varying philosophies of the century might explain the likeness in different ways: one, as participation by man and nature in a universal spirit of feeling; another, as attribution by man to nature of feelings of his own; and yet another, as sympathetic recognition of various type representations along a scale of increasing complexity of feeling. But all seemed to agree on the literary expression of the likeness by what was to be called fallacy.

We have seen, also, that with an increase of sensibility it became proper to feel these likenesses in delicate degrees rather than to see them in the large; and this change meant at first an inclusion of increasingly small objects: of animals and more birds and then, increasingly, of modest flowers. The change was twofold: it meant, first, that even the smallest natural objects participated in the universal spirit (getting away from magnitude standards of judgment), and second, that the artist's discrimination and sensitivity was supposed to be increasingly fine—he could sense and sympathize not only with live bird and mouse, but even with the feeling motion of the unfolding petals of a flower.

Upon the flower, style could easily grow and turn. The flower could still be representative of type—the rose of love, the vi'let of tim'rousness; it could represent also how deeply a universal feeling expresses itself in the simplest, most natural, things; and it could, further, call upon the immediate sensing of the poet by its refinements to touch, to smell, to sight, its intricacy of form and variety of coloring, and its part in a pattern of surrounding atmosphere.

To such refinements had the flower brought the fallacy of Tennyson. The personifications of Darwin, of Wordsworth, of Keats, and their representative qualities of color as gaiety, smallness as shyness and fear, turned into Keats's smarting rose, Shelley's light along the grass, and, in sum,

> All he had loved and moulded into thought,
> From shape, and hue, and odour, and sweet sound.

So too, the spirit of Tennyson's crimson rose expresses itself in *odorous sighs,* and his *merry bluebells* have a stanza of their own atmosphere. And further than this, in Tennyson, this sort of adjectival emotion is not the exception of his predecessors, but the rule. Most of the bestowed emotions of his early writing are enforced by adjectives: the emotions rise not from the standard representations of the object, but from associations of its color or texture.

Some of the objects themselves are new. Note in the list already quoted the broken sheds, the salient springs, the things forked, horned, and soft. These are taken direct for atmosphere, not for standard association. Some of the objects are familiarly pathetic, but here in different ways: the *star* is *sad,* and why? not because stars look sad in general, but because this one sets at twilight (there is the sad association) and in a land of reeds (there is the individually picturable atmosphere); the wind's amorousness comes here with its odorousness; the usually happy dawn is tearful here because it is glimmering, as seen through tears. The brook loves, not out of a general brookish spirit of love, but because of its own sensuous enjoyment of matted cress; the springs have hearts not to sympathize with, but to be seen as pulsing. Entire poems, like "The Dying Swan," are concerned with the senses of a combination of natural objects in their feeling moods.

It was noted at once by the critics that this Tennyson had been much impressed by Keats, and Tennyson himself spoke of Keats as the great poet of the time. In the range of the pathetic fallacy it is possible to recognized not only Tennyson's enlargement of a tendency in Keats, but also a close imitation of phrase. *Sad place* is characteristic of them both, and the *mourning* of gnats, and the river's enjoyment of *cresses.* But more basic to their common style than these was their agreement on the frequent use of the word *sweet.* This they shared with Shelley, as Tennyson shared *dim* too with Shelley; and sweet and dim, as used now where once were *pleasant* or *happy* or *smiling* or *gay,* indicate the basis of diction and thought on which Tennyson in his early years was building so firmly: the language and world of direct simple sensation as connotative of the fullest meanings and feelings.

Though after 1850 the richness of this language was never to be so great in Tennyson, some use of the kind of fallacy he had created survived. *Beat, happy stars, turning with things below, ... the soul of the rose went into my blood, ... the cobweb's threaded tears; the glad and songful air, . . . the silver year should cease to mourn and sigh*—there are many lines like these in, for example, "Maud" and the "Demeter" poems, where quality establishes feeling. "In Memoriam," 1850, as the central poem of his career, maintains as central too the Keatsian sensibility in the fallacy. It provides not only such characteristic phrasing as *The low love-language of the bird,* and *The red fool-fury of the Seine,* but some that is particularly memorable, as the day's *dull goal of joyless gray,* and especially in "In Memoriam" style, as *High nature amorous of the good.*

Let us look a little further at this central philosophical poem for a wider view on Tennyson's attitude toward "bestowal" terms. The poem begins by addressing Love, in traditional fashion. Its second stanza group then addresses, even more in the convention, an old funereal yew tree, eighteenth-century sign of mourning. Will the yew mourn for Hallam? No, that is not to be the question, but rather,

> . . . gazing on thee, sullen tree,
> Sick for thy stubborn hardihood,
> I seem to fail from out my blood
> And grow incorporate into thee.

So Tennyson's physical terms immediately assert themselves, making the relationship between human and natural a sensed physical likeness and bond. *Sick,* not *sad,* is the word; and *incorporate,* not *sympathetic.*

Then, in the third group, the fallacy is bitterly faced: Nature is a phantom, *A hollow echo of my own;* in the eleventh, the echo is equably accepted: *Calm is the morn without a sound, Calm as to suit a calmer grief;* and finally that resolution is reached in the one hundred and thirtieth, which Scott and Shelley also reached, that whether the mourning, whether the sympathy, is direct or no, the mourned one's spirit has a place in nature—*Thy voice is on the rolling air*—and the love is the greater for being mingled with nature and with God, resting on the final metaphor of the

> ... one far-off divine event
> To which the whole creation moves.

It is to be seen, in other words, that Tennyson evolved, even here, no new philosophy of world or art to fit and sustain the style he had begun with so forcefully. As his feeling for the yew began in this poem a vein he did not finish in, for want of theory how, so too his poems before 1850 began a style he did not thoroughly sustain. Nevertheless, this style was an actual creation in the small realm of the pathetic fallacy and makes a milestone of the 1840's as the decade when shape, hue, odor, and sweet sound came into their inheritance. So fully did they inherit that any one poetic device can merely suggest the fullness of their power. These were the years when emotion itself became less abundantly stated, as *grey,* as *bright,* as *sweet* acquired the ability to state them by indirection. This was the poetry which told of the natures of girls by reference to seasons, bees, clouds; which mentioned spring and the voices of birds and let one draw one's own conclusions concerning mood; this is the poetry which first was lyrical about the form and color of the Kraken without any explicit remark about his emotional significance; this first asked *only* to know how the woodbines blow, and rested a major poem and story upon the refrain,

> I heard the ripple washing in the reeds,
> And the wild water lapping on the crag.

This was, in other words, a poetry and a time which was discovering and using a primacy in a new set of words, though it was not conscious of the theory of the use. The pathetic fallacy, long a central device, was to suffer some change and some diminution.

Those modern critics who are so far converted to this spirit that they wish to define even poetry itself in these terms of *qualities* usually look to Keats, not Tennyson, as the major innovator.

I expected him to be so in the realm of the fallacy: I expected from him less fallacy first of all, and especially less standard eighteenth-century fallacy: but this was expectation based on the somewhat distorting view of a later century. Keats's new sensibility reached just a little way into a standard material which he used wholeheartedly. Tennyson's altered in quality by more than half, and in quantity too by half, the characteristic appearance and abundance of the device. Keats, with Shelley in this respect, however great their differences in others, marked the pathetic fallacy with the notion: that which is sweet, soft, cool, *feels*. Tennyson half transformed the fallacy by his early and full acceptance of this notion. The long century of increasing discrimination within textures, temperatures, colors, in Tennyson's bestowal of feeling received first enough emphasis to be taken for a pattern of expression. Here the emotions and object qualities sustained a long, firm parallel, an extended implied or explicit simile, joined equally well by bestowal of feeling on quality or by its objectified reverse, so that river could have feeling, or feeling could flow like river; and the power of the constant parallel at last made explicit device of bestowal less necessary to Tennyson, and so less frequent.

This matter of the decreasing frequency of the pathetic fallacy in Tennyson, even before the 1840's, may be associated with that other poet greatly admired by Tennyson, Scott. As we have seen, Scott was strong in his transference of the fallacy to a status of artistic rather than naturalistic reality, as he was strong in reduction of its use in numbers. The frequency in the "Lay of the Last Minstrel" was just half that of the standard, and the character of the devices was strictly traditional. It may be thought upon first consideration that the narrative nature and the ballad nature of the work had some effect upon bestowal usage. But the fitting to the standard by Beattie's "Minstrel" and by the Wordsworthian "ballads," as well as the extra-abundance in Burns, would indicate that feeling nature was not necessarily hindered by the necessity for action. Scott's style was his own; and it was, as one might hope for the sake of clarity of attitude, clearly condemned by Wordsworth, who preferred Beattie, he said,[6] and Dorothy Wordsworth, who thought Scott's work a compendium of falsity in expression.[7]

By Tennyson, by Rossetti and Morris, by Ruskin, Scott's work was not condemned; it was deeply praised. All these men, with so much of artistic attitude in common, were raised in youth on Scott and for many years knew poetry in general through his poetry; knowledge of his style was one of the things they shared.[8] Scott had died in 1832, but his writing had not had to wait to live. It was, rather, itself eagerly awaited by readers-aloud; it was immediate fireside material, and it was material to be acted out and recited by boys of ten who had just a decade or so in which to grow up to be Pre-Raphaelites.

It is noteworthy that, of these four who expressly state their fondness for Scott, three should be poets who followed his lead in the strong decrease in use of the pathetic fallacy, and the fourth the critic who by his denunciation of the device gave it its later technical name and fame. A unanimity in mid-century, then— a clear concerted motion in poetry, after a hundred years of the pathetic power, toward a lessening of its force,—this unanimity and direction were part of a natural progress of thought, but they were guided directly, however unawares, by the frugality of one poet. The figures are these: the Pre-Romantic standard of frequency of the bestowed feeling was once every fifty or sixty lines. Scott's frequency was once in one hundred and twenty. Tennyson's average was once in eighty-five or so, but the poems written

---

[6] *Letters: Middle Years,* ed. De Selincourt, II, 631.

[7] *Ibid.,* I, 425 (and 417).

[8] See *Alfred Lord Tennyson, A Memoir,* by His Son, p. 12; Ruskin, *Praeterita* (Cabinet Edition), Vol. I, chap. i, pp. 13–14; also pp. 443–448; and *Modern Painters,* Vol. III, Pt. IV, chap. xvi, §36, where Ruskin praises Scott especially for lack of pathetic fallacy; *Dante Gabriel Rossetti; His Family Letters,* ed. William Michael Rossetti, I, 59–60; and William Morris, *Works,* Vol. XXII, note on reading, pp. xvi, xxii, xxxi.

after 1830—that is, all except the "Juvenilia"—equal Scott's spar-sity of device or exceed it. The Rossetti and Morris frequencies likewise range about once in one hundred and ten to twenty. Three other major poets of the new century, Hopkins, Meredith, and in his way Housman, were to use the device with just such frequency, from once in a hundred to once in a hundred and fifty lines. Again, it seems, some sort of balance and agreement was established in an unconscious consensus of poets, and a standard of usage presents itself. The major quantity from about 1840 on is just half that for the preceding century, as our poets represent it. The pathetic fallacy, whether by Ruskin's prescription or its own nature, was cut in two.

Now what remained of the fallacy—what was its nature? what was the Pre-Raphaelite notion of the pathetic in the natural world? Granting the preëminent force of Keats as well as Scott in influence on these poets, one looks for two phases: the fallacy of quality, as notable in Tennyson, and the earlier standard fal-lacy of representative sympathies.

This standard of gay lark and sighing wind had survived not only Wordsworth and Scott alike, and Keats in all his elabora-tion, but even the ministrations of the Annuals. Tennyson in *happy morn, joyful dawn, merry bird, doleful wind, sighing winds, merry bells, cheerful day, blissful clime, glad year, happy shores, happy stars, weeping rose, moaning waves,* and *smiling Nature,* and some few more like these, many of them used often, heartily maintained the standard. Even here, the objects bells, stars, and shores have something of a new ring to them. Rossetti supplies *the blithe bird; rook grieving; merry morn; spring merry;* and Morris, the *happy place; flies . . . unafraid; The primroses are happy; This merry summer-tide;* their traditional phrases are visibly fewer, and even, in surrounding context, less traditional, since they are often used ironically, in the ballad variety of contrast rather than in standard sympathetic correspondence. But still, comparing these to Scott's, one sees a certain continuity. Seasonal emotions persist; all their summers smile. The dew of flowers, especially roses, is still equivalent to tears. Winds still sigh in trees. *Nature* shows emotion. A notable contrast may be that between Scott's scene and Keats's-Tennyson's-Morris' *place;* either may be sad or happy, and the latter seems to be a substitute for the former, but its implications are very different. *Scene* suggested hills, vales, fields, trees; *place* suggests detail of leaves and flowers. A stream can run through both place and scene, a wind can sigh through place and scene, and seasons can emote on place and scene. So these more fluid phases of nature provide the bond, between one century's pathetic fallacy and the next, in declining degree.

As for the fallacy of quality, the silver-soft-and-sweet, it was maintaining its new, Tennysonian, preëminence. One of Rossetti's adjectives was *iron: Yearned loud the iron-bosomed sea,* and *Oh the wind is sad in the iron chill.* Similar adjectival phrasings are his *Dumb tears from the blind sky,* his *ere the gleam/Of autumn sets the year's pent sorrow free,* and Morris' *Four spikes of sad sick sunflowers stand; Wind, wind, unhappy! thou art blind; the happy golden land; the happy poplar land;* and *the elm-tree flowers fell like tears.* Iron, blind, golden, sick, these are the new adjectives of emotion, which give emotion a new substantial existence because of their qualities.

They suggest too—do they not?—some sort of waywardness of reference when viewed in contrast to the *happy lark.* For example, these are human physical, as well as emotional, traits bestowed on nature. *Sick, blind,* how much complexity of anguish these bear with them. *Iron, golden,* how differently, and with what malice of inversion, then, are the two metals used. If even in these few pages one has become accustomed to a major body of standard statement, with the light and shade of individual variety playing over it, how much more deeply accustomed must Victorian readers have been to the century of human philosophy which gave voice to that standard statement. And how irregular these new words are, then. Buchanan's "fleshly"[9] epithet is to be sympathized with in view of just two adjectives employed in a single device: the *blind* wind, the *sick* sunflower. So the close view in poetry intensifies the wider vision.

The fleshly and physical element in the pathetic fallacy showed only barely in the *sweet* and *faint* of Shelley and Keats, and then more strongly in some lines of Tennyson which stressed the senses rather than the sympathies of things. His *beating hearts of salient springs* was an example, and, in the light of Rossetti's verse, other lines as yet unquoted provide a major word as term for the stress:

> And Nature's living motion lent
> The pulse of hope to discontent.

Nature's living motion is important to the poets of his time, for the discriminations of Nature's aspects have become so great, the motions so various, they are obviously not all parallel and sympathetic and read in; they go on in independence and in spite of human bestowal, it appears, and the feelings of physical nature are naturally physical feelings.

Therefore we come, with Rossetti and Tennyson, to this new major word and concept within the fallacy, the word and concept of *pulse*. It takes the place of the eighteenth-century *face* of nature and the Wordsworthian *breath*. The living motion which was for Wordsworth a motion of spirit is now more organic. The metaphor, as it is stronger, also sets nature more strongly apart as its own organism intrinsic to its own spirit. Here are some of Rossetti's phrasings of this pulse metaphor:

> Where the inmost leaf is stirred
> With the heart-beat of the grove.
>
> . . . blossom beat like a heart.

---

[9] Robert Buchanan, "The Fleshly School of Poetry," *Contemporary Review*, XVIII (October, 1871), 334–350.

> [the sea] ... it hath
> The mournfulness of ancient life,
> Enduring always at dull strife.
> As the world's heart of rest and wrath,
> Its painful pulse is in the sands.

Here the separate feeling:

> The blushing morn and blushing eve confess
> The shame that loads the intolerable day.

And here the similes with power that is now reversed: the natural object is the base, the human emotion the vehicle for its clarification:

> ... the sea
> Sighed further off eternally
> As human sorrow sighs in sleep.

> Until the night-wind shake the shade like fear.

> ... like the human play
> Of scorn that smiling spreads away,
> The sunshine shivered off the day.

This focus on sensed quality, which sought to strengthen sound and aspect not only by attribution of emotion but also by analogy of the sensed qualities of emotion, characterizes most vividly the pathetic fallacy of Rossetti, and, secondarily, of other Pre-Raphaelites. The device, in small, represents a new characteristic of poetry in the large; and though about that larger characteristic I have not knowledge enough to make any but standard generalizations, still the alterations in the device, item by item, suggest what should be looked for. Natural objects are connected explicitly with feelings in these ways: by conventional association; by adjectival association; by physical sense as expressed by the pulse metaphor; by use of feelings as illustrative of qualities; by opposition, with nature and man both feeling fully, but apart and often ironically. All these are phases of the pathetic fallacy, and they point to a nature more and more withdrawn from man and independent, not as personified, but as a feeling organism.

The cutting in half of the amount of fallacy also indicates such a withdrawal. At the same time, the increase of a reverse method of attribution, the objectification of feelings, especially in Tennyson, Rossetti, Swinburne, Meredith, indicates the new relationship. This device of objectification provides a major study in itself; here I mention it only as it casts the declining fallacy in relief. Its nature is suggested by Rossetti's phrase "The rustling covert of my soul." Soul, heart, mind, mood, affection, love, hate, hope, all the structures of human feeling, are dealt with in terms of the color, form, and motion of the outer world: they are objectified thus. Particularly they are objectified in this period by the current subjects of fallacy also: clouds, winds, and flowers. The standard "river of the soul" symbol which ran its course through such poetry as Wordsworth's River Duddon sonnets, now widens out and deepens into all sorts of detail of motion and fragrance which is used to clarify the nature of feeling. In fine, the stress of interest upon qualities in nature as sensed has these three effects: the decrease of the pathetic fallacy in poetry, the alteration of its nature, and the increase of the reversed attribution of physical qualities to emotional. Objectification, a subordinate device throughout the period ending with Keats and Shelley, becomes equal in amount to the pathetic fallacy for Tennyson and Browning, and double that amount for Rossetti, Swinburne, and Meredith, almost so for Hopkins. So the small devices move in the current of thought, and so Rossetti is seen to intensify to its extreme the kind of poetic statement for which Tennyson was founder, and Keats and Shelley, as they would say, "faintly," pioneers.

The course, in amount and kind, from Tennyson through Rossetti, Morris, Meredith, Hopkins, Housman, seems steady enough to justify viewing these poets as a group, as the poets of the "new" poetry. But in between are major poets who disagree: Browning, namely, and Swinburne. The former diverges by reason of his reticence, the latter by his overabundance. Browning's language, not only in the "Men and Women" poems here noted but also in his lyrics as a whole, sets him apart as poet from his contemporaries. The difference comes not simply from dramatic form, then, but may come from dramatic feeling: a constant ironic use of statement which makes first for a reduction in stated feeling, second for a reduction in the use of figures of speech for this feeling, and third, therefore, a reduction in the amount of the pathetic fallacy in particular. We have seen that up to the 1840's the standard was once in every fifty or sixty lines; after the 1840's once in every hundred or more lines; Browning's frequency is once in two hundred and eighty lines, more than a halving again of a device already halved. Further, the device declines not merely in proportion to the decline of stated feeling in general, but more, so that even in relation to the total of stated feeling it is unusually subordinate. Browning was simply uninterested in the poetic power of attribution of feeling to nature.

The brevity and convention of the attribution when he does make it reflects this lack of interest. Coursers and isles feel *pride*. That is his version of the standard association. The one phrase *far sad waters* is his version of the Pre-Raphaelite fallacy of quality. Closest to an original contribution is his use of man-made objects as feeling, his *gay fire, glad burgh,* and *melancholy little house.* Not that these were new, but that their feeling of intimacy was closely bound with human; they were between the pathetic fallacy and no fallacy at all. Browning had a line like Shelley's, as Shelley was his master,[10] which praised "The shapes of things, their colors, lights, and shades"; like the Pre-Raphaelites, he looked for interest in nature to these sensible aspects of it. But unlike his contemporaries, he did not regularly make a connection between these aspects and stated feelings. His pattern of the world was an outward pattern. He described not scene plus emo-

---

[10] William Clyde De Vane, *A Browning Handbook,* p. 11.

tion from it, but scene plus people in it; he combined faces with mountains, and towns with rivers as wonders of the world, and death and Euripides with flower and sunset as things to take the heart from unbelief. His outer world was an object of vigorous sense perception, much less poetically participant in men's feelings than heretofore.

Swinburne, though he too had a line like Shelley's and Browning's on "All form, all sound, all color, and all thought" (the distinguishing Victorian line), emphasized the sound beyond the rest of these, with a repetition of *sighing* and *wailing* world, flower, wind, and sea which carried his fallacy back to the abundance of the pre-'forties. His general statement of feeling also was excessive for his time, and his frequency of fallacy was in proportion to that excess. Aside from the strong emphasis on sound of sadness and mourning, Swinburne's usage was much like that of his confreres. He, too, reversed the process of attribution, clarifying soul by sense. He made identifications which once would have been personifications: *the earth was a sweet wide smile,* rather than smiling. He elaborated qualities of nature by qualities of feeling, as in his *seed-pods* dry as the heart of a dead man. His skill of combination, however much fostered by alliteration, made for statement rare till then:

> Beyond the hollow sunset, ere a star
> Take heart in heaven from eastward, ...
> And all the night wherein men groaned and sinned
> Sickens at heart to hear what sundawn saith....
> O white birth of the golden mountain-side
> That for the sun's love makes its bosom wide
>   At sunrise, and with all its woods and flowers
> Takes in the morning to its heart of pride!

The so-called classical element in Swinburne shows itself with grace in the fallacy in lines such as *O Phosphor, from thy pride of place.* The negative aspects appear in much *waiting,* adjectives like *sick* and *bitter,* and the praise of *hate* as in "In the Bay," which at least seemed negative to his time. And further, he some-times took the pains to deny the fallacy itself, saying of the dead, for example, that *They are loveless now as the grass above them/ Or the wave.* But on the whole, though excessive both in number of fallacies and often in elaborateness of statement, Swinburne's poetry expressed a view, a technique, a stress on the conditioning quality of simple sense which was greatly like that of Morris and Rossetti and their followers.

Of the followers there is less new to be said. The Tennysonian language had truly established itself in the Pre-Raphaelite terms, and though the pathetic fallacy diminished steadily, after Swin-burne, back to the Victorian standard of once in a hundred or a hundred and fifty lines, it kept to its regular channel of nineteenth-century, as distinguished from eighteenth-century, phrasing. The adjective was its key and clue, the *wind* its major object, and melancholy its major feeling, with rivers, flowers, and birds also of importance.

It is probable that parallel to this current of diction there was running another, a Wordsworthian poetry. It is probable, there-fore, that for many Victorian poets the abundance of the fallacy did not subside, and its character continued to be one of direct philosophical bestowal of feeling on natural objects, the implied connecting metaphor being that of the *breath* of feeling. Brown and Bridges are two, for example, who may represent this other course. On the other hand, the increasing use of the title "Impres-sions" in the latter half of the century would indicate an increas-ing attention to qualities, to shape and color rather than to love and hate, and thus a further growing away from the Words-worthian spirit. The truth of the matter I do not at present know. At any rate, it seems that the poets I have looked into as perhaps representative are at least representative of the one trend: the decline and the qualification of the fallacy.

Meredith's phrasing of fallacy in the "Ballads and Poems of

Tragic Life" has not the distinction of his writing apart from the device. *Woeful* and *angry seas, rapturous birds* are to be found, and *The heart of horror of the pinnacled Alp,* and, most notably, *in fear/Western day knocked at his door.* He uses Phoebus, as Swinburne Phosphor. His contribution to a new activity and spirit of nature is not through the fallacy.

Hopkins, more equably, says what he has to say best in the device as well as out. What he has to say very deeply is the pervasiveness of God throughout the world, and like his predecessors he takes this pervasiveness in terms of qualities. He has got back to an emphasis on spirit, yet has put it in the word of sense. He takes the breath and pulse together. *What is all this juice and all this joy? A strain of the earth's sweet being in the beginning....* He speaks of *Spring's universal bliss and ecstasy through all mothering earth;* he is intent upon this spread of feeling to all being, and so uses traditional terms in the most meaningful way. One could call his the purest sort of continuance of the fallacy, since it is used with both convention and heart. Also, he continues the use of the adjectival kind, the lines familiar, yet altered just by *surfèd: And thicket and thorp are merry/With silver-surfèd cherry.*

Does Hopkins take and use instinctively? No, the "Ribblesdale" poem indicates; he has a clear opinion on the nature of the device, and has made a poetic statement of it tenderer than Scott's or any till now.

> Earth, sweet Earth, sweet landscape, with leavès throng
> And louchèd low grass, heaven that dost appeal
> To, with no tongue to plead, no heart to feel;
> That canst but only be, but dost that long . . .
>
> And what is Earth's eye, tongue, or heart else, where
> Else, but in dear and dogged man?
>
> . . . this bids wear
> Earth brows of such care, care and dear concern.

This conception of the attribution is neither so literal nor so bound to literary powers as Scott's. Even in giving Earth leaves and low grasses and denying it heart, Hopkins speaks indirectly, as if this very earth heard and felt the affection with which he speaks. With a certain assumption of familiarity, like Blake's, yet with the added sensory force of the period, he is the poet who theorizes with most richness of past and present on his bestowal of feeling. His interest is centrally in qualities, in likeness and unlikeness, in beauty of relation; his use of the traditional fallacy, then, is a friendly acceptance; but in addition he is able to express in a new mixture of traditional terms the philosophy of the new attitude toward objects.

> Not of all my eyes see, wandering on the world,
> Is anything a milk to the mind so, so sighs deep
> Poetry to it, as a tree whose boughs break in the sky.

The "poetry" which the boughs sigh to the mind is neither sympathy nor strict association: it is the poetry of quality, form, and relationship. It is the poetry which Wordsworth had taken thought of in his prose note on the oak tree almost a hundred years before, but which his poetry seldom managed, and which only now, with the aid of Ruskin, was coming into active life.

Housman's use of the fallacy in the next decade, the last of the century, was, as might be expected, less re-creative, more repetitive. Its frequency was just as scant as Hopkins'. Its standard was Victorian, with the stress on *sighing air, wind,* and *poplars,* this latter shift from general tree to specific poplar being itself standard. The line *'Tis the old wind in the old anger* sums up the usage. One pleasant variation, a little apart from the device as we observe it, is the attribution of the powers of wise and reasoning speech to *aspen* and *blackbird,* as heretofore mainly to rivers if at all. The pure Housman virtues, whether one considers them moving or monotonously trite, display themselves in one elaborated version of the fallacy. It is a version, from the *Shropshire Lad,* which can indicate to us, more vividly since we know its ancestry, just what Housman contributed to the line of poetry: a restatement; a simple directness; a filling out, by the sheer presence of colors and flowers, of an accepted poetic notion.

> In my own shire, if I was sad,
> Homely comforters I had:
> The earth, because my heart was sore,
> Sorrowed for the son she bore;
> And standing hills, long to remain,
> Shared their short-lived comrade's pain.
> And bound for the same bourn as I,
> On every road I wandered by,
> Trod beside me, close and dear,
> The beautiful and death-struck year:
> Whether in the woodland brown
> I heard the beechnut rustle down,
> And saw the purple crocus pale
> Flower about the autumn dale;
> Or littering far the fields of May
> Lady-smocks a-bleaching lay,
> And like a skylit water stood
> The bluebells in the azured wood.

Earth's sorrow and the likeness of bluebells to skylit water are of equal importance as comfort, and that is the compromise which Housman reflects. His further reflection, that in the city men are too unhappy to sympathize, is less up to his time. It is Wordsworth's fallacy, not Browning's. But his stress upon the azured wood as itself a comfort speaks for the poetry of his contemporaries. The texture and color of such discriminated specialities as beechnut and lady-smock have come so to participate in a complexity of feelings that their names are used in poems to strengthen and enforce the old simply stated emotion.

The old stated and bestowed emotion has less force in itself by Housman's time than it had for Gray. We have seen, through twenty poets within a century and a half, the steady and clear decline of the device of bestowal. That a trend of thought can show itself so precisely in the work of major poetic and original minds is itself illuminating. These at which we have looked are, so far as we are apt to guess, the least likely to follow any line of phraseology that is set by the times, yet of them all only Tennyson is a major innovator in matters both qualitative and quantitative. There are two clear groups, one before Tennyson, one after, with strong bonds of style between. In each of these there is an exception, as far as amount of use goes: Scott looks forward in this respect, and Swinburne back. On the whole, the device of the fallacy seems to exist formally by reason of its vigor in the thought of the time; and its career, however wonderfully altered in context by its poets, moves along firmly within a whole career of thought. Its motion, I should surmise, is quicker in the major than in the minor poets. The great body of Victorian, as of modern, poetry may well be fuller of the fallacy than Housman and Hopkins. But that is speculation, for we know little of the relation of innovation to major use in the poetry of any time.

The position of some modern poetry is surprising. The continued decline of interest in the pathetic fallacy seems perfectly natural. What Housman used less than Wordsworth in the way of attribution, we would seem to want to use less still. The scantness in the work of Eliot and Jeffers therefore seems certainly to participate in the fading of a way of thought. The frequency in Eliot's poetry up to 1925 is once in almost three hundred lines, and the fallacies' nature is mild and unpretentious. A boat responds *gaily,* light is *sad light,* a *moon smiles.* Beyond these the figures have a shade of other sorts of figures in them, the *fear in a handful of dust,* for example, and the *wrath-bearing tree.* Jeffers' in *Solstice* are as minor, in spite of the great parallel emotions in the poem. They are almost echoes of an earlier world. We perceive in technical terms in these poets the validity of a changing feeling toward the world.

The surprise to me is in the work of the Imagists and in the choices of those who have written in this century on "pure poetry," "objectivity," and "the thing in itself." Here I can only doubt, pending further investigation, that the work I thought to be representative is representative after all. At least "in itself" it brings up new questions about the position of Imagism and the "purity" of sense presentation of which critics like Max Eastman are so fond.

Through the decline of the pathetic fallacy, and through the growth within the fallacy of the use of qualities, colors, temperatures, textures, the increasing power of interest in "the thing in itself" has made itself apparent. "Vivid presentation to sense" is the slogan,[11] and, as Professor of Lowes has written, "What does it look like, sound like, feel like, taste like, smell like?—that formula is the very sea-mark of our utmost sail."[12] This was the import of Imagism: the quality of the thing, not our feelings about it. The word, for Amy Lowell, was "externality."[13] The question, What *is* the thing in itself? has been asked the more rarely as faith in sense perception has been literal.

Yet the frequency of fallacy in the representative collection, *Some Imagist Poets,* of 1915, is once in sixty lines, equal to the strong pre-Tennysonian. Moreover, since the collection's total statement of emotion is only half the earlier standard, the bestowal of emotion is double by proportion. The bestowal is fondly done. The terms are simple: *love, shame, happy, weeping,* are the emotions, with *pride* most frequent; but the objects are newly discriminated, so that the phrases themselves do not fall tritely. *Wind, mist, smoke, rye, fireflies, deer, irises* suggest that, within the device at least, the Imagists have simply extended again the realm of objects. Adjectives are still important, as in Aldington's *I know that the white wind loves you,* and Law-

---

[11] See, for example, Eastman's *Enjoyment of Poetry.*
[12] John Livingston Lowes, *Convention and Revolt in Poetry,* p. 8.
[13] S. Foster Damon, *Amy Lowell: A Chronicle,* p. 296.

rence's *A fine proud spike of purple irises.* There is also distinction in Lawrence's phrasing *I wash you with weeping water.* Lawrence, in fact, is the major employer of the fallacy; but H. D. is the only one to ignore it, and it would be interesting to know further whether her attitude did consistently set her apart from her confreres. On the whole, the Imagist theory precludes the pathetic fallacy implicitly and explicitly, as one reads it today, yet the Imagist practice provides for the device in loving abundance, centering evidently with such heart upon the objects of nature that even stated feeling seems natural to their "sensed presence." It is not merely the long Wordsworthian line, for all its survival in our time, that preserves the pathetic fallacy to us, then. It is not just our "Georgian," in contrast to our postwar poetic attitude, that maintains the pride and joy of winds and flowers. The modern poetry of object quality is still, too, a poetry of object feeling.

Whether this retention of device is by earnest purpose or by absentmindedness, I do not yet know. Certainly, the average run of current issues of *Poetry, A Magazine of Verse,* exhibits with all its loyalty to the fallacy not much vigor or new concept in its use. The issue for March, 1940, has a frequency of once in ninety lines, which is higher than any work observed since Tennyson, except Swinburne's and the Imagists'. The phrasing is conventional: *hopes of day, proud* and *frightened horses, sighing grass.* Most outstanding is the figure for the eyes of wild things as *flames of anger or surprise.* The distinguished writing in the magazine is that very writing which, ignoring the device, involves the relationship of men and objects in new terms.

Yet, on the side of heartfelt poetic acceptance of the device, there is George Moore's *Pure Poetry,* published in 1924. It is a very textbook of the pathetic fallacy. It is the charming text, also, of the poets and critics of the "world of things," of whom perhaps Eastman spreads his doctrine farthest. For "acquaintance with the thing," for "vivid sense presentation," they turn with pleasure to Moore's anthology as prefaced by Moore's crystallizing argument. Here they find the poetry of things, not of man's feeling about things, or theorizing, or soul-seeking, or cosmic searching, or attributions, particularly and expressly not Wordsworth's, but just the pure objective world of the things themselves. Tenable or not as this theory of pure poetry may be, one does not expect from it to find, as one does find, the thick pathetic atmosphere of the poetry used by Moore in illustration. The poetry he selects from Blake through Swinburne (who is his "modern"), for example, contains at least three times as much pathetic fallacy as does the representative work which we have observed by the poets included. There is more even than the Pre-Romantic standard. The frequency, in these selected poems, of once in thirty lines may very probably, therefore, reflect a selecting attitude which favors it.

What is this attitude which has persisted into the first quarter of the twentieth century? It signifies, evidently, an increased reliance upon the objective force and being of natural objects, a reliance which increases too, rather than decreases, the statement of powers of feeling in objects. The Pre-Raphaelite and strong modern trend is toward a stress on qualities and textures and forms which relegates the attribution of vaguer "feelings" to the background or oblivion. But we have in Imagism and in some "pure poetry," perhaps, the revival of an attitude closer to Keats and the exercises of Southey and Hunt, a poetic view so intent upon emotions that its firmest "objectivity" requires emotions *in* the object.

The problem of the pathetic fallacy, then, is not a stale one, or a rhetorical one, and it has not, even in the terms in which Ruskin expressed it, been solved. It is central to the total philosophy of the times and to the literary convention of the times. It involves problems not only of inauguration and elaboration of devices, but of inauguration and elaboration of attitudes. The question whether attribution of human emotion to natural objects is poetically valid depends upon whether it is valid in current thought; and as the metaphysics, so the poetics of it changes. We have had a good two hundred years of it in view here, and it is clear that the device which was a century old and more when Ruskin rebelled against it is not yet to be referred to as antique. These points are clear also: that a single major device may have an extraordinary persistence through the work of even the most original poets; that the turning point of this one, in both nature and amount, was reached practically by Tennyson before it was reached critically by Ruskin; that its decline is traceable through the poetry of the Victorian period into the poetry of influence in our own day; that it nevertheless plays a major part in one body of current poetry; that it represents, and is a clue to, that changing relation of man to nature, and of art to objects, about which there has been so much discussion. Within the unit of the device, containing an object and an attributed feeling, these emphases have been discerned: first, the outward representative aspect of the standard object, its *face;* second, the shared sympathy of an increasing number of objects, their spirit, or *breath;* third, the organic force of objects to feel in terms of sensed qualities, the power of adjective within noun, its own generation of emotion or *pulse*. These are notable distinctions in relationship within a device; but they are more than this—they are distinctions which provide definitions for poetry. The poetry of the eighteenth century was that of mirror and model, the poetry of ideal aspect. The poetry central in Wordsworth was that of sympathy, the stimulation and generalization of feeling. The poetry of Tennysonians was of qualities and their atmospheres. Such generalizations hold within the device and they hold for total relationships between poets and objects, and they hold, further, through the defining metaphors made by the poets themselves. Poetry is "a species of painting with words," said Goldsmith; it is the "breath and finer spirit of all knowledge," said Wordsworth; it is the "odour and colour of a rose to the elements which comprise it," said Shelley. Such are the qualities of representative aspect, the breath of sympathy, and the qualities of sense, respectively, as they make for poetry.

The fallacy, as it participates in these views, has a natural poetic place and force. It is the stronger, over a period of time, as it is used instinctively, out of need of just such metaphor. But, further, it was given, at one major turn in its career, an explicit place in theoretical discussion also, by Ruskin; so that it has, as a label, a technical sound and discarded virtue quite apart from its poetic life. Victorian poetic theory casts light upon the career of the fallacy, and in return the fallacy, and the objects it relates to, make clearer some of the references of the "naturalistic," the "pantheistic," the "transcendental" philosophies which controlled them.

III. PROSE

IF THERE WAS, in the 1840's, the major change in poetry which the pathetic fallacy seems to reflect, in quantity as well as quality, questions arise respecting the philosophical nature of the change. What philosophy produces in poetry a lessening statement and attribution of emotion and an increasing power of special adjectives? Eighteenth-century *aspect* had a clear connection with associationism and the psychology of vision. Wordsworthian *breath* is an effective if vague metaphor for what he meant by both the naturalistic sharing and the transcendental bestowing powers of emotion and 'mind. As, in the Victorian period, nature gathered its forces and grew sympathetically apart from men, so the savor of its qualities came closer, and when Ruskin wavered between a love for *all* objects and a love for useful objects, between vision and recognition, between surface and form, his was a "moralistic aesthetic," right enough, but it was also part of a wavering of view which was to change Impressionism into the structures of Cézanne. Further into the realms of the isms I would not explicitly at present go, for two reasons: first, our level of observation here is that of minutiae, and they have their own power of implication; second, those writers whose level of observation is the philosophical have, in respect to the poets with whom we are here concerned, usually ignored the minutiae, even when they are contradictory to the generalization; and therefore to the duties of observer I do not dare as yet add the duties of referee.

So in asking what clear thought if any is behind the break in fallacy form, why the new consciousness of it and label for it just after its change, I do not conclude that Wordsworth and his poets up to the 'forties were *x*-ists, while Tennyson, Ruskin, and the Pre-Raphaelites were *y*-ists, as they assuredly were, but I set together two anecdotes. I do not ask the large question of what

Wordsworth and Ruskin thought of the universe, but merely the middle-sized question, What did they see when they looked around?

At fourteen, Wordsworth says in his prose note to a youthful poem, "An Evening Walk," he saw an oak.

> And, fronting the bright west, yon oak entwines,
> Its darkening boughs and leaves, in stronger lines.

This is feebly and imperfectly expressed, but I recollect distinctly the very spot where this first struck me. It was in the way between Hawkshead and Ambleside, and gave me extreme pleasure. The moment was important in my poetical history; for I date from it my consciousness of the infinite variety of natural appearances which had been unnoticed by the poets of any age or country, so far as I am acquainted with them; and I made a resolution to supply, in some degree, the deficiency. . . . I will conclude my notice of this poem by observing that the plan of it has not been confined to a particular walk or an individual place,—a proof (of which I was unconscious at the time) of my unwillingness to submit the poetic spirit to the chains of fact and real circumstance. The country is idealized rather than described in any one of its local aspects.[1]

This moment of "consciousness of the variety of natural appearances" was important in literary history, if not for the brand newness of that consciousness among eighteenth-century poets, at least for the firmness of the resulting resolve. "Infinite variety"—that meant an increasing number of objects to be recognized as noteworthy for poetry; "natural appearances"—that meant Wordsworth's favorite phrase about "the eye on the object"; and note that the spot was in the way between Hawkshead and Ambleside—it had a literal location. This was the passage, the first of it, which led Dewey to make a naturalistic paragon of Wordsworth:

Here is a definite instance of transition from the conventional, from something abstractly generalized that both sprang from and conduced to incomplete perception, to the naturalistic—to an experience that corresponded

---

[1] Prose note to "Evening Walk," *Complete Poetical Works,* ed. A. J. George. Wordsworth's prose notes consist of those he prepared for the edition of 1850 and those he gave Miss Fenwick. See Dowden's Aldine Edition of the poems for discussion of notes.

more subtly and sensitively to the rhythm of natural change. For it was not mere variety, mere flux, he wished to express, but that of ordered relationships—the relation of accent of leaves and boughs to variations of sunshine.[2]

"Yon oak," I think, had not so complex a function. It presented a striking outline of dark upon bright, and it gave Wordsworth "extreme pleasure"—*that* was philosophically important.

Important, too, was the conclusion of the passage, so often ignored. The scene was idealized, not limited to local aspects. Wordsworth, he said, was unwilling to "submit the poetic spirit to the chains of fact and real circumstance." How, then, the naturalist's variety and flux? The sight of the oak was important to Wordsworth's poetry for the two facts he states, not merely the one. Consciously he recognized a variety of natural appearances; unconsciously at the time, but with fuller understanding later, he preserved some of his time's method of seeing natural appearances, as unbound by the chains of local fact, as idealized. The oak pattern, then, is significant to him, not for ordered relationships within itself, in its own form, its "accent of leaves and boughs," but rather for its ordered relationship with the perceiver, its stimulus of pleasure, the feelings and thoughts which as natural appearance it calls up. So the poem the note introduces is a quite orthodox piece of descriptive verse in its time, and its stress is on the emotional effects of the things described. So, too, the prose note of a few years later, dealing in finer detail with the slant of boughs and the color of leaves, yet serves to introduce a poem, "Lines Written in Early Spring," the terms of which are those of the pathetic fallacy and "what man has made of man."

Still a decade later, in his note to "The White Doe," Wordsworth was praising "bestowal" as he philosophized about it. Still, in the next decade, while his Essay Supplementary to the Preface of 1815 made its famous pronouncement on the lack, between "Paradise Lost" and "The Seasons," of images which might indi-

---

[2] John Dewey, *Art as Experience*, p. 154.

cate either eye-on-object or "the spirit of genuine imagination," his definition of the working of imagination in that very Preface stressed its conferring and abstracting powers which enabled the object to react upon the mind in new ways, its dealing with things "not as they are" but as they exist to the senses and passions; not things, but the "inherent and eternal properties of things." And in the next decade: ... "our business is not so much with objects as with the law under which they are contemplated."[3] And finally in the 1830's, in that period of his confidence and acceptance, his reasons for the idealizations in "Yarrow Revisited": " ... it is next to impossible entirely to harmonize things that rest upon their poetic credibility, and are idealized by distance of time and space, with those that rest upon the evidence of the hour, and have about them the thorny points of actual life."[4]

The view of the oak in Wordsworth's youth was a view, then, prolonged through the years of his writing. It was as important for its duration as for its impact. However his theories altered from part to part, the oak maintained its place and shape before his imagining eye: with all other selections from the infinite variety of natural appearances, it gave "great pleasure," not as it was, but "as it existed to the senses and passions," idealized, and without its thorny points of actual life.

Wordsworth's oak, for all its dark outline against the bright sky, was most important for the human feelings it aroused and shared in; these were its poetic life.

Now Ruskin, too, tells of a tree he saw, a few years later in life, "a small aspen tree against the blue sky."

Languidly, but not idly, I began to draw it; and as I drew, the languor passed away: the beautiful lines insisted on being traced,—without weariness. More and more beautiful they became, as each rose out of the rest, and took its place in the air. With wonder increasing every instant, I saw

[3] *Letters: Later Years,* ed. De Selincourt, I, 184.
[4] *Ibid.,* II, 580.

that they "composed" themselves, by finer laws than any known of men. At last, the tree was there, and everything that I had thought before about trees, nowhere.

The Norwood ivy had not abased me in that final manner, because one had always felt that ivy was an ornamental creature, and expected it to behave prettily, on occasion. But that all the trees of the wood (for I saw surely that my little aspen was only one of their millions) should be beautiful—more than Gothic tracery, more than Greek vase-imagery, more than the daintiest embroiderers of the East could embroider, or the artfullest painters of the West could limn,—this was indeed an end to all former thoughts with me, an insight into a new sylvan world.

Not sylvan only. The woods, which I had only looked on as wilderness, fulfilled I then saw, in their beauty, the same laws which guided the clouds, divided the light, and balanced the wave. "He hath made everything beautiful in his time," became for me thenceforward the interpretation of the bond between the human mind and all visible things.[5]

These were the thoughts, he says, which gave rise to the writing of *Modern Painters*. In some fundamental positions they were very like Wordsworth's, and we may look at these more closely; but in eyesight they were thoughts of a new world of form. There had broken with startling significance upon Wordsworth's sight the vision of "an infinite variety of natural appearances," mainly at the level of objects—daisies, lakes, birds, oaks,—as they struck the feelings. The shock to Ruskin was at a closer level of discrimination. Granted the flower, granted the tree as of emotional importance, see suddenly their inward form: their proportions, texture, color, line; the motions of clouds, divisions of light, balances of wave; and all these as, too, of emotional and poetic importance. God or Nature is not merely infusing feelings through things; the things have an organic force and pattern for beauty, and an art of sensible form, as God directs them.

Wordsworth was walking, Ruskin was sketching, when the two made their respective discoveries. This difference in concentration itself had its effect on what was to be seen. It is significant, therefore, that so many poets of the Victorian period were paint-

---

[5] *Praeterita* (Cabinet Edition), II, 252–253.

ers and sketchers (by interest if not by vocation, like Hopkins), whereas so many poets of Wordsworth's time had walked earnestly in the hills of England. Things were now to be looked at more closely. Stones, leaves, and flowers could be taken home and studied for grain and texture. The amateurs of the see-God-in-a-flower period were coming, through the popular influence of the Annuals, into a more glorified philosophical position, and the long-forbidden streaks on the tulip now were to be viewed as having a prime significance.

Note how plain description of a scene, even one not remembered as permanently significant by the two poets, differs between them. Wordsworth's includes many factors; Ruskin's stresses one of these. Wordsworth's, from a letter in 1821:

It is a charming region, particularly at the spot where the Eden and Emont join. The rivers appeared exquisitely brilliant, gliding under rocks and through green meadows, with woods and sloping cultivated grounds, and pensive russet moors interspersed, and along the circuit of the horizon, lofty hills and mountains clothed, rather than concealed, in fleecy clouds and resplendent vapours.[6]

Ruskin devotes as many words to a river alone:

... alike through bright day and lulling night, the never-pausing plunge, and never-fading flash, and never-hushing whisper, and, while the sun was up, the ever-answering glow of unearthly aquamarine, ultramarine, violet-blue, gentian-blue, peacock-blue, river-of-paradise blue, glass of a painted window melted in the sun, and the witch of the Alps flinging the spun tresses of it forever from her snow.[7]

Or, to make a contrast in passages of the same descriptive, or view, structure, in foreign lands, and in color, here is one of Wordsworth's from Ireland and one of Ruskin's from the Apennines.

The Sun though not above the horizon had filled the East with purple and gold—One mountain opposite of Majestic size and varied outline was steeped in deep purple, so were the battlements and towers of a Ruined

[6] *Letters: Later Years,* I, 6.
[7] *Praeterita,* II, 262.

castle at one end of the small town—the Ruin is one of the finest we have
seen in Ireland—the stream was visible in the valley, blue smoke ascending
from the thatched cottages, and in different parts of the valley forming
itself into horizontal lines resembling vapour, and on the sides of the hills
also, all was quiet and beautiful, glowing light and deep shadow.[8]

So much color is rare in Wordsworth—this is an exceptional description by him, while the first quoted was typical,—but it is
closest to Ruskin's usual style, as exemplified by a like view:

The clouds were rising gradually from the Apennines, fragments entangled
here and there in the ravines catching the level sunlight like so many
tongues of fire; the dark blue outline of the hills clear as crystal against a
pale distant purity of green sky, the sun touching here and there upon their
turfy precipices, and the white, square villages along the gulf gleaming like
silver to the northwest; . . .[9]

Ruskin's further reference in this passage was to Turner and to
more color and outline; Wordsworth's, to an old woman's song
and a religious conflict. This difference in association, the one
with artist's forms, the other with human feelings, carries through
all such prose writing of the two men. I have chosen passages
not exceptional, but representative—except for Wordsworth's
Irish one, which brings his style as close as it can come to Ruskin's
—in respect to view description, at which Wordsworth was much
more practiced than Ruskin.

   In spite of the exhibited likenesses, then, the resulting differences are characteristic of two ways of seeing, even from a hilltop.
Most of Wordsworth's objects are associated objects: streams and
clouds in sound and shape have suggestion of infinities, which
this poet always required; cultivated plains went with human
simplicities; lofty hills, with lofty feelings and thoughts; the ruin,
with the traditional and literary moods of every cultivated man.
The purple and gold, and the lines of smoke like vapor, are near-
est to discernment of form and color. Both passages are written

---

[8] *Letters: Later Years*, I, 416–417.
[9] *Praeterita*, II, 227.

with feeling and sensitivity, and are "beautifully" done, as Ruskin would say too; their basis of value for Wordsworth is their long connection with lasting human values of simplicity and lofty spirit in nature.

Ruskin's concern for the river is totally its color and the flash of its impression on the mind, as he writes it here. His clouds, his hills, his villages, these are all Wordsworthian objects in outline, but beyond the outline the natures change: they move not into human connection but into their own more specific qualities— *like tongues of fire, clear as crystal, a pale distant purity of green sky,* these are the amplifications to be made. And while Wordsworth's village suggests by its smoke the peaceful activity of its inhabitants, Ruskin's villages are *white* and *square,* they are facts of color and shape, as they might be painted.

A change in the focus of the eye, a change in what the heart wants to see: that is the basis of difference between Wordsworth and Ruskin, and between the times they represent. The eye wants to look at last within the outlines of objects, and past their class features; and the poet wants to tell what is found there—he is going to have to deal with phases *within* objects, two colors shading together, the points on either side of a leaf, the grain of wood and stone respectively. Ruskin's river suggests the language: the language of adjectives and of correspondences between sense impressions. We have seen just the glimmer of this language in the changing pathetic fallacy. Ruskin's autobiography *Praeterita* is its autobiography too. Ruskin loved Scott the describer of things,[10] was fascinated by the excesses of Shelley's "Sensitive Plant" and decided it was on exactly the wrong track,[11] was puzzled by Keats,[12] accepted the Pre-Raphaelites as men of true vision,[13] and so learned gradually, as poetry did, the language of the adjective of sensed quality.

---

[10] *Praeterita,* III, 448; (and *Modern Painters,* Vol. III, Pt. IV, chap. xvi, §36).
[11] *Praeterita,* I, 156.
[12] *Ibid.,* II, 221.
[13] "Pre-Raphaelitism," 1851.

The Wordsworthian oak, then, resided on a different plane of vision from the Ruskinian aspen. But their two supporting philosophies were not so far apart. Neither man followed a unified system of thought; both have been accused of contradicting themselves, not only at different times of life, but in successive paragraphs. Both, in any event, had a strong heritage from eighteenth-century aesthetics and common thought, which gave them these points in common: a belief in certain objects as enduring and "worthy" because of certain major characteristics (such as the loftiness of mountains as uplifting to the spirit and therefore working toward moral good), and a belief in "beauty" as "good," because of its psychological basis in pleasure and the ennobling human feelings. Fundamental here, therefore, is the persistence, especially through the persuasive and representative powers of Sir Joshua Reynolds' *Discourses,* of objects as (1) living up to ideals established universally, and (2), in special cases, having special values of beauty or sublimity because of association of aspect, magnitude, form, and use, with uplifting human emotions, primarily established in pleasure.

It is not surprising therefore to find Ruskin writing, throughout *Modern Painters,* of *beauty* and *poetry* in terms of feelings, as Wordsworth would, and with something of Reynolds' "idea of central form," of the intention as the ideal of the object, though all the while he was against Wordsworth's kind of idealized form. The fact of the matter was that there were in Ruskin's mind at once a justifiable hangover of theory from the past and a clear impression of how he liked to look at things. He made a very solid beginning at theorizing on his own account, but increasing attention to problems of social improvement made him cling to more and more of the old psychological-uplift-by-uplifting-objects-and-forms idea.

It is noteworthy that in the sections of the essay dealing with the pathetic fallacy and surrounding material he seems most at ease, and in his own empirical and historical terms. This Part IV of Volume III is entitled "Of Many Things"—it does not force him into any pattern of thought. It concerns mainly style in the realization of nature, the place of painting, the history of attitudes toward landscape. It does not do much defining, but it has a remarkably noticing eye out for its own order of "facts." The thought runs something like this: that Reynolds is wrong about "High" and "Low" painting; it depends not on methods or materials, but upon the aims of the artist. A truly great style involves subjects associated with deep passions, love of beauty, sincerity, and invention. The sum of these is the sum of the human soul and therefore "great." The false ideal seeks religious or physical beauty; the true ideal is naturalistic, it seeks things as they *are*. The Ideal must be *real* and *whole*. Turner draws "absolutely and universally." It is the Imagination that sees things thus, the size, source, eternity, as well as the outward view, of the Alps, for example. The modern world sees new things never seen before: blue mountains, clear lakes, and ruined castles. There has been an extraordinary change in human nature—"a passionate admiration of inanimate objects." What is in the object?—colors and such qualities are, but feelings are not (and to say so is fallacy). The Greeks dealt with either unimaginary objects or divine powers, as subjected to human service. The medieval times had a sense of the unaccountable in nature, and of inaccurate formalisms. The modern age is bleak and in the "service of clouds." Scott, and to a degree Wordsworth, have sight of the truth of things, not merely feelings. There is a science of the Aspect of things, as well as of Essence, and Turner is its master. And:

> . . . as the admiration of mankind is found, in our times, to have in great part passed from men to mountains, and from human emotion to natural phenomena, we may anticipate that the great strength of art will also be warped in this direction; . . ."[14]

[14] *Modern Painters*, Vol. III, Pt. IV, chap. xvi, §22. And see Vol. III, Pt. IV, chaps. i, ii, vii, x–xviii.

So, in the welter of old terms of elevation and association, what is good style and what is good subject, about which Ruskin was none too sure, though positive, this major fact stands out: the recognition of a new central interest in things as they *are,* and that means, essentially, as closely as they can be seen by the eye. This is where Ruskin and Wordsworth deeply differed. Wordsworth feared constantly the "tyranny of the eye" that might put transient before eternal things; he spoke of immediate sight as an enemy to the imagination; his imagination was grounded in "the plastic, the pliant, and the indefinite":[15]

I mean to say that, unless in those passages where things are lost in each other, and limits vanish, and aspirations are raised, I read with something too much like indifference.[16]

With all his sensitivity toward the nature of objects, he did not feel for their own form and life as Ruskin did. A letter of 1805 contains a passage revealing most expressly his sympathetic but nonstructural feeling for realities.

We are in the midst of the realities of things; of the beauty and harmony, of the joy and happiness, of living creatures; of men and children, of birds and beasts, of hills and streams, and trees and flowers; with the changes of night and day, evening and morning, summer and winter; and all their unwearied actions and energies, as benign in the spirit that animates them as they are beautiful and grand in that form and clothing which is given to them for the delight of our senses.[17]

See how much motion, activity, and spirit Wordsworth has infused into the eighteenth-century world of aspects; but see also how secondary, by metaphor and stated dependence, he makes form and quality.

Ruskin rescues them; he goes back to eighteenth-century *aspect* and makes a new virtue and power of it; for this reason he stated in *Modern Painters,* as I quoted, that there could be a science of

[15] Preface, 1815.
[16] *Letters: Later Years,* II, 134–135.
[17] *Early Letters,* p. 527.

Aspect as well as of Essence, and that art was that science. Its tool was not the microscope and not the dissecting knife, but that *eye* which Wordsworth had somewhat mistrusted for its sight of what he had taken to be "accidents"; these accidents were now the things to see, the "clothes" were the heart. Here is a passage from Ruskin remarkably parallel to Wordsworth's in structure and tone, but indicating a new sort of looking; directly, as his descriptions do indirectly.

I was absolutely interested in men and their ways, as I was interested in marmots and chamois, in tomtits and trout. If only they would stay still and let me look at them, and not get into their holes and up their heights. The living inhabitation of the world—the grazing and nesting in it,—the spiritual power of the air, the rocks, the waters,—to be in the midst of it, and rejoice and wonder at it, and help it if I could,—happier if it needed no help of mine,—this was the essential love *of Nature* in me, this the root of all that I have usefully become, and the light of all that I have rightly learned.[18]

And this was the method of the looking and learning:

On fine days, when the grass was dry, I used to lie down on it and draw the blades as they grew, with the ground herbage of buttercup or hawkweed mixed among them, until every square foot of meadow, or mossy bank, became an infinite picture and possession to me, and the grace and adjustment to each other of growing leaves, a subject of more curious interest to me than the composition of any painter's masterpiece.

A flower is to be watched as it grows, in its association with the earth, the air, and the dew; its leaves are to be seen as they expand in sunshine; its colours, as they embroider the field, or illumine the forest. Dissect or magnify them, and all you discover or learn at last will be that oaks, roses, and daisies, are all made of fibres and bubbles; and these, again, of charcoal and water; but, for all their peeping and probing, nobody knows how.[19]

The two men are agreed, as through the word "peeping," that the dissections of chemists and botanists are not for them; but on what the eye may properly see for its own good they differ, then. The purpose of Wordsworth's prose was to stress the great

[18] *Praeterita*, I, 142.
[19] *Ibid.*, II, 348–349.

emotional sympathies with simple people, words, and things; while a purpose of *Modern Painters* was

. . . to explain to myself, and then to demonstrate to others, the nature of that quality of beauty which I now saw to exist through all the happy conditions of living organism; and down to the minutest detail and finished material structure naturally produced.[20]

Thus far in fifty years had scientists, as Wordsworth predicted, brought new fact into the material of art.

Now we come to the specific stylistic devices which the views entailed. We have seen how way of looking, way of describing, and way of justifying are involved together; and the way of statement in words in poetry is no less involved. Both Wordsworth and Ruskin wrote in detail of techniques of expression and the places of figures of speech. Though some contemporary writers have explained much of Wordsworth's theory of poetic language by what they believe to be his basic dislike or rejection of metaphors and figures,[21] actually he and Ruskin agreed as closely in their pleasure in good, feeling, figurative speech as on any single point. For both, the test of a figure was its sincerity, the fullness of the feeling it rose from; what separated them was simply the difference in their notions of what things one could justly feel sincere about. Ruskin wrote of metaphor as "legitimate fallacy," and praised the powers of personification. Wordsworth looked with favor on "tender similitudes," and analyzed his own abundant use of imagery in "The Excursion."

Not long before Ruskin's warning against the fallacious use of pathetic attribution, it is not surprising, therefore, that Wordsworth had made such a warning also.

We have had the *brow* and the *eye* of the moon before, both allowable; but what have we reserved for human beings, if their features and organs etc.,

---

[20] *Ibid.*, pp. 335–336. Ruskin also wrote that "the greatest thing a human soul ever does in this world is to *see* something, and tell what it *saw* in a plain way."—*Ibid.*, Vol. III, Pt. IV, chap. xvi, §§23–24. See this passage further for relation to Wordsworth.

[21] For example, the studies by Srikumar Banerjee and Marjorie Latta Barstow on Wordsworth's theories of poetic diction.

are to be *lavished* on objects without feeling and intelligence? You will, perhaps, think this observation comes with an ill grace from one who is aware that he has tempted many of his admirers into *abuses* of this kind; yet, I assure you, I have never given way to my own feelings in personifying natural objects, or investing them with sensation, without bringing all that I have said to a rigorous after-test of good sense, as far as I was able to determine what good sense is.[22]

Further, in that sonnet of Gray's which he held up in the Preface as a bad and famous example, Wordsworth condemned exactly the sort of fallacy to which Ruskin objected, the birds "in amorous descant join," and "The morning smiles its busy race to cheer" sort of line, in which the feelings in proper eighteenth-century fashion are beheld upon the face of nature rather than felt by direct sympathy through the heart. So too the objects in Ossian were found "false" because dislocated from stated human response.[23] Wordsworth makes this very distinction, in fact, in his own precise terms, in the 1815 Preface, when he finds one simile of "dew as tears" false, one true. The false is Chesterfield's: dewdrops are the tears of the sky mourning the departure of the sun. It is just not so, says Wordsworth; it is *fanciful,* it gives surprise, but there is no essential truth to the idea that sky weeps for sun. The true is Milton's: the sky, after Adam, weeps for the fall of man. Nature does have that sympathy; on fundamentals, such as good and evil, all things feel as one; at such a philosophical depth the pathetic fallacy, though Wordsworth does not use that term, is valid for him. Such the test for sincerity and good sense. It enables Wordsworth to consider and refer to as one of his best descriptions of nature ("in which beauty majesty and novelty, nature and art, earth and heaven are brought together with a degree of lyrical spirit and movement which professed

[22] *Letters: Later Years,* I, 436–437. It is interesting to note how Lord Kames had made somewhat the same distinction for what he called "personification" or "prosopopeia" (see also Hoskyns, Goldsmith, etc.), which, along with "figure of speech" and "hyperbole," covered the pathetic fallacy. The rhetorical terms did not precisely fit the new idea. Henry Home, Lord Kames, *Elements of Criticism,* pp. 329–341.

[23] Essay Supplementary to the Preface of 1815.

Odes have, in our language, at least, rarely attained")[24] his "Eclipse of the Sun" which attributes joy to sun and other objects of nature as tritely as possible, but in the service of his own feelings. It makes for the high frequency and established standard of his bestowal of feeling, throughout his work.

Ruskin had not this standard. He required connection with feeling, but not in this particular one-two relation of stated sympathy. He himself in his prose and occasional verse willingly let flowers unfold their petals with delight, for example, but their delight was theirs (or his) in their form and color, and not necessarily a philosophical bond of feeling. The feeling, in its modern insistence, he thought, unjustly subordinated the object; and this was just what Wordsworth expressly did. Particulars, Wordsworth said, were "bricklaying" before the main structure; his objects were "illustrations"; they derived influence not from what they *are,* as Ruskin would have wished.

Throughout, objects . . . derive their influence not from properties inherent in them, not from what they are actually in themselves, but from such as are bestowed upon them by the minds of those who are conversant with or affected by those objects. Thus the Poetry, if there be any in the work, proceeds whence it ought to do, from the soul of Man, communicating its creative energies to the images of the external world.[25]

Ruskin's "passionate admiration of inanimate objects" gave much more value to the objects themselves, and therefore found the Wordsworthian standard of emotion excessive. He thought the emotion, so essential to his predecessor, often "unconnected with any real power or character in the object, and only imputed to it by us."[26] The fallacy was one not merely of willful fancy, as Wordsworth would have admitted, but also of an excited state of the feelings, and thus "pathetic."

Now we are in the habit of considering this fallacy as eminently a character of poetical description, and the temper of mind in which we allow it, as

[24] *Letters: Later Years,* I, 65.   [26] *Modern Painters,* Vol. III, Pt. IV, chap. xii, §4.
[25] *Letters: Middle Years,* p. 705.

one eminently poetical, because passionate. But, I believe, if we look well into the matter, that we shall find the greatest poets do not often admit this kind of falseness,—that it is only the second order of poets who much delight in it.[27]

In this second or reflective order Ruskin put Wordsworth, Keats, and Tennyson, not making any distinction between them. Through all this writing of his there is remarkable his recognition of the "atmosphere" of the device, its place in its time and its reason for being. Such recognition was relatively rare, in application to rhetoric, however strongly it was growing in general discussion.[28] It will be remembered that here the author proceeded to talk about classical and medieval views of objects, all the while pointing up by these both the "modern" and the new view he would have take its place. This modern, what was its nature?—it was made up from emotion, mystery, doubt.

The temperament which admits the pathetic fallacy, is, as I said above, that of a mind and body in some sort too weak to deal fully with what is before them or upon them; borne away, or over-clouded, or over-dazzled by emotion; and it is a more or less noble state, according to the force of the emotion which has enduced it.

. . . the curious web of hesitating sentiment, pathetic fallacy, and wandering fancy, which form a great part of our modern view of nature.

. . . exactly in proportion as the idea of definite spiritual presence in material nature was lost, the mysterious sense of *unaccountable* life in the things themselves would be increased, and the mind would instantly be laid open to all those currents of fallacious, but pensive and pathetic sympathy, which we have seen to be characteristic of modern times.[29]

This, then, is the fault of the romantic for Ruskin: its emotion, which has a strain of the mysterious, the vague, the hesitating, the wandering, which is borne away or overclouded, which will not deal fully with that which is before it. This is the fault of the

---

[27] *Modern Painters,* Vol. III, Pt. IV, chap. xii, §6.

[28] As historical perspective became greater, literary criticism by men like Matthew Arnold and E. S. Dallas centered more and more on writing in relation to its period and culture, with a function in the social good of the times.

[29] *Modern Painters,* Vol. III, Pt. IV, chap. xii, §8; chap. xiii, §13; chap. xiv, §7.

fallacy: that it moves away so quickly from object quality to human sympathy. This is the fault of Wordsworth as second-rank: that he loves his thoughts and feelings more than the objects with which they are concerned. The point is not to say that rock or waterfall "haunted me like a passion," as Wordsworth has said in characteristic phrasing. The human love of objects has a greater preëminence; it is not *like,* but *is* a passion; "the point is to define how it *differs* from other passions,—what sort of human, preëminently human, feeling it is that loves a stone for a stone's sake, and a cloud for a cloud's."[30]

Here is the aesthetic, and here is the "sake" which is to make so much trouble for the aesthetic. What is the stone for its own sake? what is art for its own sake? what are words for their own sake?—all these have been problems of the century since. The essential disagreement between Ruskin and Wordsworth is exactly on this ground of "sake" and this ground of the connections of feeling. The pathetic fallacy represented a view which saw the object for the passion's sake, and so for Ruskin it was false; for him the passion rose for the sake of the object, and the two together were beautiful. What, then, was this object other than Wordsworthian felt tree and sympathetic flower? The object as Ruskin sees it is the sake he means; and we have surmised that it is an object of color, design, pattern, organic form. Fortunately, we have more than surmise to go on in summary, for Ruskin makes his own explicit contrasts, to establish with some finality the values he has been talking about.

I had, in my little clay pitcher, vialfuls, as it were, of Wordsworth's reverence, Shelley's sensitiveness, Turner's accuracy, all in one. A snowdrop was to me, as to Wordsworth, part of the Sermon on the Mount; but I never should have written sonnets to the celandine, because it is of a coarse yellow, and imperfect form. With Shelley, I loved blue sky and blue eyes, but never in the least confused the heavens with my own poor little Psychidion. And the reverence and passion were alike kept in their place by the con-

---

[30] *Praeterita,* I, 183.

structive Turnerian element; and I did not weary myself in wishing that a daisy could see the beauty of its shadow, but in trying to draw the shadow rightly, myself.[31]

In this statement there is every aspect of contrast between two views which we have been attempting to follow. First of all there is some agreement: the whole century was earnest to remember the heavenly spirit behind objects, whether that spirit was in terms of Nature, God, or Soul. From these, in fact, the objects philosophically took their worth; that was agreed in Words-worth's Prefaces, Shelley's Essay, and over and over painstakingly in the *Modern Painters* and succeeding works. But then there are disagreements, for the reason that a new standard of value, of goodness and truth as well as of beauty, had been coming to light. It is represented in Ruskin's words here by *coarse yellow, imper-fect form, blue sky and eyes,* and *shadow rightly.* It could justly be called an aesthetic standard, except that the very use of that term has long confused and even concealed the facts it covers, by implication of oppositions between goods, truths, and beau-ties. The standard could be called artistic, though that term raises problems in the painting-music debate which are perhaps here not pertinent. It is at least a standard which a critic of Ruskin's theories in their widest application calls characteristic of him, a standard of "fact or material substance, rather than ideal essence," which makes truth "the faithful statement either to the mind or the senses of any fact of nature," and which holds "a reverence for what really is—for truth . . . the great artistic necessity."[32] What this comes to, in the small range of our study, is concrete instance, which weights the whole. Ruskin prefers snowdrop to celandine, though both speak of God, because of color and texture; and he prefers rather to consider the shade than to sympathize with the feelings of a daisy. This is exactly the position of choice which the poets of his time were taking,—had already begun to take

[31] *Praeterita*, p. 182.
[32] Henry Ladd, *The Victorian Morality of Art*, pp. 29–30, 31, 58.

before he mentioned it,—in respect to their own celandines and daisies. He wrote, then, for a trend of thought, at is beginning.

How close to the beginning, is indicated by the general criticism of the preceding century. Were the objects and images used by the poet *worthy?* That was the one great concern of the critics over objects. The pathetic fallacy was worthy, just so long as it combined worthy objects with worthy passions. A mountain mourning for some lost love, for example, was worthy, for it had magnitude, it was uplifting, it suggested by its aspect the noblest passions. One finds this very interpretation, with its consequences, most neatly in *Tom Jones,* wherein Tom wishes he were at the top of the hill:

" . . . for the solemn gloom which the moon casts on all objects, is beyond expression beautiful, especially to an imagination which is desirous of cultivating melancholy ideas."—"Very probably," answered Partridge; "but if the top of the hill be properest to produce melancholy thoughts, I suppose the bottom is the likeliest to produce merry ones, and these I take to be much the better of the two."[33]

All through the criticism of Wordsworth and Shelley, for example, such was the sober point of view. Wordsworth's associations were for long considered not worthy. Anna Seward, who, as Professor Monk makes clear in his pleasant study of her, had the purest eighteenth-century sensibility, accepted with passionate delight the romanticism of objects and their effects—pictorial scenery, the rough sublime, Ossian, Scott, and the appeal of woods and mountains to the heart; but she, like other critics, resented Wordsworth's "capricious" linking of daffodils to laughter, and called the effort an "egotistic manufacture of metaphysical importance upon trivial themes."[34] Obviously these trivia had to be seen as more important before they could be seen as colored and shaped.

---

[33] Henry Fielding, *Tom Jones,* Bk. VIII, p. 10. Quoted by Kenneth MacLean in *John Locke and English Literature of the Eighteenth Century* (New Haven, Yale Univ. Press, 1936), p. 57.
[34] Samuel Monk, in *Wordsworth and Coleridge,* ed. Earl Leslie Griggs.

Feeling, in all its current power, had to do that leveling, and Hazlitt justly attributed the best of the work to Wordsworth's muse, though he still held out for the fixity of some associations of sublimity.[35] Two or three comments to be found in the random writing of Shelley and Keats have a bearing on the changing situation of objects after Wordsworth, though most of their concern is with matters of feeling and idea. By 1811 the notion of feeling flowers had reached Shelley:

Perhaps the flowers think like this; perhaps they moralize upon their state, have their attachments, their pursuits of virtue; adore, despond, hope, despise. Alas! then do we, like them, perish; or do they, likewise, live forever?[36]

This was just about the Wordsworthian situation, and Shelley's descriptions from mountaintops were pretty much Wordsworthian, too. He had just one of water with a little more texture to it, and notably more fragrance to his flowers; but he explicitly stated that his interest was not in things.

. . . in this have I long believed that my power consists in sympathy—and that part of imagination which relates to sentiment and contemplation. I am formed, if for anything not in common with the herd of mankind, to apprehend minute and remote distinctions of feeling, whether relative to external natural or the living beings which surround us, and to communicate the conceptions which result from considering either the moral or the material universe as a whole.[37]

So the emphasis has not yet come down to what the eye can see closely. Romantic feelings, distances, and mists are more important than the outlines of things; but still *bright* and *fair* are the words that Keats wants brighter and fairer,[38] and *sweet* is one of the ten major words in the dictionary;[39] so that, through feelings,

---

[35] William Hazlitt, *The Spirit of the Age,* 1825.
[36] Carl Grabo, *The Magic Plant: The Growth of Shelley's Thought,* p. 43, quoting a letter of 1811.
[37] Shelley, letter of December, 1817; *Letters,* ed. Roger Ingpen, II, 574.
[38] *Letters,* ed. Forman, II, 382.
[39] That is, among the dozen words most used by the poets of the time, as concordance countings indicate these. See Bibliography for concordances used.

the new discriminations have at least a little begun. Further, we have a hint from Southey, surprisingly, that there was more experimenting than was meeting the eye. His Commonplace Book contains "ideas and studies for literary composition"; these include practice "Images"; and the Images are of such kind as "Water, like polished steel, dark, or splendid," and "Flags. I saw the colors in a bright sky flowing like streams of color with dazzling vividness."[40] These likenesses, these similes on the basis of sense impression, are in the direction in which the "like" will eventually be omitted, and in which the "correspondences" and analogies of Imagist thought will be of prime importance. Their presence in the poetic mind of the early nineteenth century suggests that Ruskin's and Tennyson's eyesight may have had some more specific ancestry than has been observed or looked for.

With such few hints of new object status, we come back to the 1840's, to Ruskin's time, and to Tennyson, Browning, the Pre-Raphaelites, Hopkins, to see what the contemporary poets were contributing in the way of theory to the position which Ruskin had taken, on, apparently, such meager literary grounds. They seem to have given the position immediate foundation and extent.

Tennyson saw as Ruskin saw, and wrote in that way earlier than Ruskin, but with little guiding theory to go by. He was nearsighted; he saw things closely and distinctly, or else in a mist. There was for him, as Mr. Nicolson says, no middle distance.[41] He had available, then, two major lines of expression: a profound accuracy of sense perception, and a sweeping blended sort of generalization. Both were meaningful to his time, but the generalization was the easier and more in demand, evidently, as he grew older. For him the two went together well, and he had few qualms about the "microscopic view" as such—that view which troubled his contemporaries as being perhaps a little ir-

[40] Southey's *Commonplace Book*, ed. J. W. Warter (4 vols.; London, 1851), Fourth Series, pp. 4–5.
[41] Harold Nicolson, *Tennyson*, pp. 135–136, 278–279.

reverent. He would say, on looking through the microscope, "Strange that these wonders should draw some men to God and repel others. No more reason in one than in the other."[42] Yet he himself had to suffer the praise and blame of both, the some with their obsession for accuracy upon which the Victorian "aesthetics of recognition" was founded, and the others who still, as they had in Wordsworth's work, found *bees* and *woodbines* too particular.[43] In other words, the continued "spirit in eternal things" and the newly recognized blackness of spring buds were growing along together, and Tennyson had good place for both; but his contributions in the latter line are what concern us here: the colors, the textures which made his language seem for the young men of the mid-century an entire new language of poetry. He expressed interest in *Modern Painters* more than once,[44] and some of its standards of accuracy were his own.

For example, note the descriptive passages in his letters and journals: they are few and concentrated. He did not, like Wordsworth and Shelley, cover a scene from a height in a careful framing sweep, or relay the effect upon his feelings of branches interlaced against the sky. A characteristic notation from his journal of a tour into Cornwall, 1848, is this:

> July 6th. Went to Land's End by Logan rock, leaden-backed mews wailing on cliff, one with two young ones. Mist. Great yellow flare just before sunset. Funeral. Land's End and Life's End.[45]

This is imagistic notation. It has broken into scene, for the sake of items, for facts of number, color, Turnerian atmosphere, and the larger suggestions of these which by the time of the twentieth-century Imagists could afford to be implicit altogether. It is notation like the experiments of Southey, of items and likeness of sensed quality, not of association and literal emotional connection.

[42] *Alfred Lord Tennyson: A Memoir*, by His Son, p. 102.
[43] Harold Nicolson, *Tennyson*, pp. 113–115, quotes Lockhart's review of 1833.
[44] *Memoir*, pp. 223, 277 (praise of chapter on *clouds*).
[45] *Memoir*, p. 275.

Interest in likeness of qualities was leading into the correspondence and interchange of senses which was to be so characteristic
of later poetry. Tennyson was able to say that "the violins spoke
of light" and to describe a pearl color in "The Lady of Shalott"
as "cloud-white." A "Mr. Heath, a famous lawyer, . . . said it was
absurd to explain a fixed colour as pearl by the most variable hue
in the world, that of cloud, . . . declaring still between his teeth
that, for his part, he thought poetry ought to be sense."[46] That is
a hint of the great new problem of words in English poetry:
what new meaning is to be central.

Further, there is hint in Tennyson of the kind of association
and memory which build in the unconscious, halfway between
the standard associational ties of Wordsworth and the individual
stirrings of Proust. He writes of "dim mystic sympathies with tree
and hill reaching far back into childhood . . . my own youth and
half-forgotten things. . . ."[47] The emphasis on cloud, dimness, the
half-forgotten, is partly of the Romantic tradition, and partly
occasioned by the limitations of his own sight, as both of these are
part of a new situation: given a closer view into things, their
colors and textures, where no clear representations have been
built up, how is one to name one's response? Granted, by this
time, that daffodils are connected with laughter, what still can be
said for the "yellow flare" of sunset? The response in feeling
terms *is* dim, is cloudy, is associated with things half-forgotten,
for the very reason that the discriminations of quality have begun
to reach a stage past that of the discriminations of response. So
cloud and exact detail went together in the Tennysonian diction,
as his use of the pathetic fallacy has already suggested; and so
what Tennyson recognized in Byron and Shelley is to be recognized much more strongly in him, that they, "however mistaken
they may be, did yet give the world another heart and new pulses,
and so we are kept going."[18]

---

[46] *Ibid.*, p. 90.   [47] *Ibid.*, p. 172.   [48] *Ibid.*, p. 141.

Browning, because his focus was so directly on the nature of man, had less to contribute on the nature of objects, as his almost complete ignoring of the problem of the fallacy would indicate. Also, his literary background in Quarles's *Emblems* was part of his whole leaning toward emblemizing—a view of objects with which we cannot here be directly concerned, though its progress in the nineteenth century was of major importance. But what Browning did have to contribute at random on the status of scenes and things was in accord with the trend. First of all, he got a good deal from the old-line associationism, of "suitability" of scene to subject, from Lairesse, to whom he devoted one of his "Parley-ings."[49] To the degree that he wrote "scenes," then, they were most antiquely proper to their theme, as Pippa's morning, and Roland's gloom. Scenes, however, are quite unimportant to his letters, unless they have people in them; and though he reflects both the current faith by his idea that a catalogue of lovely things is a recognition of God, and a current doubt, especially after Darwin's 1859, about the face of God in nature, his middle course was the treatment of objects, if not as symbols, as "properties."[50]

Secondly, in his letters to Elizabeth Barrett, Browning touched upon some of the Pre-Raphaelite problems. Was poetry in everything?[51] Was Browning's poetry *misty* and obscure and vague, or a subtle association of likes and unlikes new to an age which sought to deal mainly in likes?[52] Is *meandering* a good word in relation to sound, and *simmering* for quiet? Miss Barrett thought so.[53] Browning thought he had solved the problem of seeing what was to be seen. He quoted the critic who said that if three poets should go to a wood to write, one would read books on the wood before writing, one would write from stock associations, and Browning would sit down and look the wood over first.[54] That was a magnificently simple statement of a value, but it did not

---

[49] William Clyde de Vane, *Browning's "Parleyings,"* pp. 222–225, etc.
[50] De Vane, *A Browning Handbook*, quotes letter, p. 104.
[51] *Letters of Robert Browning and Elizabeth Barrett Browning, 1845–1846,* I, 45.
[52] *Ibid.,* I, 80; II, 414.   [53] *Ibid.,* I, 134.   [54] *Ibid.,* II, 559.

answer the central question—what would he choose to look at?
It is misleading if it suggests he would look at the trees. More
honest and explicit is Browning's own comparison of his view
with Tennyson's. The comparison is vivid, and exactly true to
the visions as the use of fallacy has suggested them, and may well
serve as summary, from Tennyson's point of view, of the new
poetry and its material:

> We look at the object of art in poetry so differently! Here is an Idyll about
> a knight being untrue to his friend. . . . I should judge the conflict in the
> knight's soul the proper subject to describe: Tennyson thinks he should
> describe the castle, and effect of the moon on its towers, and anything but
> the soul.[55]

The effect of the moon, not on emotions and the soul, but on the
tower in light and atmosphere—that was due to become a prime
medium for poets, and so to alter perceptibly the texture of poetry.

Among the poets called Pre-Raphaelite, at least among those
who lived in Cheyne Walk in the 'sixties, with the addition of
Morris, there was a certain amount of tacit agreement about this
new kind of "truth" in poetry. The explicit principles for seeing
what was actually there, for following "the Sun's" laws of light
and shade,[56] were laid down in terms of paint rather than of language, and the Grosvenor Gallery rather than *The Germ* was
the center of debate. The course of painting from Turner and
Constable and Delacroix through the Pre-Raphaelites, the Im-
pressionists, to Cézanne is a course which provides illuminating
illustration of the changing poetic language, as light, color, and
structure were progressively looked into. We have noted the infil-
tration of problems of color into the pathetic fallacy. They are
problems already current in painting and literature: Constable's
famous discussion of *green* made clear that the color had a life
and complexity of its own;[57] the whole intricacy of one of Flau-

---

[55] De Vane, *Browning Handbook,* quotes letter of 1870, p. 384.
[56] "Pre-Raphaelitism," 1851.
[57] See *The Journal of Eugène Delacroix,* transl. Walter Pach, p. 730.

bert's works was directed toward the effect of a single color, *purple*;[58] and Baudelaire especially noted the "green and purple backgrounds" of Poe and Delacroix.[59] An entire philosophy and symbolizing rises here which takes its stresses from at once a closer look and a half-shut eye, and the world it presents seems dazzlingly new and full of possibility.

Said the *Athenaeum* in 1857, "Pre-Raphaelitism has taught us all to be exact and thorough, that everything is still unpainted, and that there is no finality in art."[60] And that is the view there was of poetry, too. It possessed a new world and a new language. In the 'fifties, as Canon Dixon remembered,

All reading men were Tennysonians; all sets of reading men talked poetry. Poetry was the thing; and it was felt with justice that this was due to Tennyson. Tennyson had invented a new poetry, a new poetic English: his use of words was new, and every piece that he wrote was a conquest of a new region . . . till "Maud" in 1855; which was his last poem that mattered.[61]

Dixon, too, heard Morris read his first poem, "The Willow and the Red Cliff," which later was destroyed.

As he read it, I felt that it was something the like of which had never been heard before. It was a thing entirely new, original, whatever its value, and sounding truly striking and beautiful, extremely decisive and powerful in execution.[62]

Lest Dixon be thought merely to be a man easily surprised, it may be well to quote two fellow poets also on Morris. Browning wrote to William Rossetti in 1858, of the "Defence of Guenevere" volume,

I shall hardly be able to tell Morris what I think and rethink of his admirable poems, the only new poems to my mind since there's no telling when.[63]

---

[58] See *The Goncourt Journals, 1851–1870*, ed. Lewis Galantière, p. 98.
[59] See Frances Winwar [Grebanier], *Poor Splendid Wings*, p. 181.
[60] Quoted in *Poor Splendid Wings*, p. 124.
[61] See J. W. Mackail, *Life of William Morris*, p. 46.
[62] *Ibid.*, p. 54.
[63] *Ruskin: Rossetti: Preraphaelitism. Papers 1854–1862*, ed. William Michael Rossetti, p. 219.

And Swinburne, of "Jason," in the *Fortnightly Review,* 1867:

Here is a poem sown of itself. Sprung from no alien seed, cut after no alien model; fresh as wind, bright as light; full of the spring and the sun.[61]

Criticism now is using the new qualitative terms, one sees. How the qualities and the objects kept on being bound intensely to soul, how "serious and elevated invention of subject" went along with "earnest scrutiny of visible facts," in accordance with the Pre-Raphaelite principles as quoted by William Rossetti, is elaborated on by Walter Pater in respect to Rossetti:

The lovely little landscapes scattered up and down his poems—glimpses of a landscape not indeed of broad open-air effects, but rather that of a painter concentrated upon the picturesque effect of one or two selected objects at a time—attest, by their very freshness and simplicity, to a pictorial or descriptive power, in dealing with the inanimate world, which is certainly still one half the charm in that other, more remote and mystic, use of it. For with Rossetti this sense of (after all, lifeless) Nature is translated to a higher service in which it does but incorporate itself with some phase of strong emotion.[65]

Our concern with the period's recognition of the *newness!* of its own style is not to learn the major nature of that style, but merely its nature as reflected in the history of the one device of fallacy, the new view of objects which lessened attribution of feeling to them and increased connection of feeling with color, shape, and quality. What is of great importance is that the change in diction which is to be noted within the device is evidently part of a change consciously made with excitement and theorizing, in accord particularly, though Tennyson's work came first, with the Pre-Raphaelite program in painting. Wordsworth and Keats had early, and without program in mind, approved the original Pre-Raphaelite painting, the Italian and German "elder Schools" before Raphael;[66] the trend became visible in the diction of

---

[61] *Fortnightly Review,* 1867. Quoted in *Collected Works of William Morris,* Vol. XXII, Introduction by May Morris, p. xv.

[65] Dante Gabriel Rossetti, *Letters,* ed. William Michael Rossetti, I, 437–438.

[66] *Ibid.,* II, 39–40, Rossetti expressed pleasure at Keats's opinion; and Wordsworth, *Letters: Later Years,* III, 1123, to Haydon, 1842.

Tennyson; and it was then Ruskin, namer and disclaimer of the pathetic fallacy, and defender of the Pre-Raphaelite Brotherhood, who was its spokesman. That Ruskin was spokesman, not merely inventor, was recognized by his pupil Morris, in ringing words. That the whole new view was not his but the time's, that there was to be remarked in the 1840's and 1850's the power of renewal and change of focus, and that Ruskin remarked it, is the point that one can hope to make, and that Morris makes well of his master.

True it is, that his unequalled style of English and his wonderful eloquence would, whatever its subject-matter, have gained him some sort of a hearing in a time that has not lost its relish for literature; but surely the influence that he has exercised over cultivated people must be the result of that style and that eloquence expressing what was already stirring in men's minds; he could not have written what he has done unless people were in some sort ready for it; any more than those painters could have begun their crusade against the dulness and incompetency that was the rule in their art thirty years ago unless they had some hope that they would one day move people to understand them.[67]

Now, with some sense of the firmness of Victorian intention and recognition in mind, let us look at what specifically the poets Rossetti, Morris, Swinburne, Meredith, Hopkins (for he was no sideline sitter in this cause) had to say of the import of objects and the value of fallacy in bestowal of feeling. The main facts are these. First, Ruskin's term "pathetic fallacy" was not often used in discussion, but explanations were constantly being made of the reasons for the device—how men naturally felt about nature. There was some hesitation over the validity of attributed feeling. Second, noting of the values of cloudiness and dreaminess continued, along with an increased interest in the powers of involuntary memory. Third, complexity of distinctions in descriptions of nature increased, inner qualities of things became more and more carefully apprehended, until the "inscape" of

---

[67] Morris, *Works*, XXII, 60, "The Beauty of Life" (1880).

Hopkins brought their organic structure and form to the solidity with which Cézanne too saw them. Here are some prose passages from the poets' letters and journals, to be contrasted with Wordsworth's elementary detail and Keats's classic richness of allusion and Shelley's "lack of eyes," and Ruskin's eager discovery. A very great deal of this prose, of Morris' and Hopkins' especially, is beautiful for its delight in detail and vigor in detail; the difficulty is not to quote it all; it outdoes the philosophers, Pater, Arnold, a hundredfold in telling what the times were about, and how, to the intensity of perception, there still clung the atmosphere of the Wordsworthian emotion and ideal, the tenderness for the fallacy, now that it was no longer central.

Rossetti wrote to Madox Brown:

I lie often on the cliffs, which are lazy themselves, all grown with grass and herbage, not athletic as at Dover, not gaunt as at North Shields. Sometimes through the summer mists the sea and sky are one; and, if you half shut your eyes, as of course you do, there is no swearing to the distant sail as boat or bird, while just under one's feet the near boats stand together immovable, as if their shadows clogged them and they would not come in after all, but loved to see the land. So one may lie and symbolize till one goes to sleep, and that be a symbol too perhaps.[68]

For Rossetti this is "symbolizing"; for Morris too it is a part of the natural imagination, and the poet's.

That thing which I understand by real art is the expression by man of his pleasure in labour. . . . A most kind gift is this of nature, since all men, nay, it seems all things too, must labour; so that not only does the dog take pleasure in hunting, and the horse in running, and the bird in flying, but so natural does the idea seem to us, that we imagine to ourselves that the earth and the very elements rejoice in doing their appointed work; and the poets have told us of the spring meadows smiling, of the exultation of the fire, of the countless laughter of the sea.[69]

Morris' interpretation in terms of human activities rather than human sympathies is noteworthy; it is part of the social trend of

---

[68] *Ruskin: Rossetti: Preraphaelitism*, p. 9.
[69] Morris, *Works*, XXII, 42.

the work of these artists, and it is easily extended to a summary explanation of the new situation of objects as such: why those who cling to the traditions of Alps are mistaken.

> I mean that the course of the fishing-boat over the waves, the plough-share driving the furrow for next year's harvest, the June swathe, the shaving falling from the carpenter's plane, all such things are in themselves beautiful, . . .

> Now, I say that there are two things to be done by the seers for the non-seers: the first is to show them what is to be seen on the earth; and the next to give them opportunities for producing matters, the sight of which will please themselves and their neighbors, and the people that come after them. To train them, in short, in the observation and creation of beauty and incident.

> What, then, is worth seeing on the earth? In one word, everything: this to love and foster, and that to hate and destroy.[70]

Morris, of course, was no better at seeing *everything* than anybody else, but he emphasized one important way that vision might widen: over the objects of social use. Swinburne emphasized another way: over objects not merely morally innocuous and trivial, such as daffodils, but also objects deeply associated with lines of association not elevating for Wordsworth's time— over "ugly" objects, over snake and cat, and an unconstructive nature. There rises here, of course, the whole problem of "aesthetic" or "decadent" values, involved in the connections between the beautiful, the valued, the socially useful, with which we cannot here be concerned except as we may note how naturally the admiration for a snake might rise after the admiration for an aspen as Ruskin wrote it down, with its "inscape," as Hopkins was to call it. Ruskin or Swinburne would say to Wordsworth, as Lafcadio Hearn explained, "Did you ever look at a snake? Did you ever study a cat?" "I beg of you," said Hearn to his audience, "to watch a snake, where its body can catch the light of the sun."[71]

---

[70] Morris, *Works*, XXII, 357 ("The Arts and Crafts of Today," 1889), and p. 426 (Address to Birmingham Students, 1894).

[71] Lafcadio Hearn, *Pre-Raphaelite and Other Poets*, ed. John Erskine, p. 150.

So Swinburne's descriptions were, as like as not, of places as "broiled, powdered, leprous, blotchy, mangy, grimy." He was a poet of adjectives, and the adjectives did not have to be pleasant so long as they had atmosphere. Here again was the characteristic combination of qualification and the effect of tenuousness. Swinburne was no original poet, as compared to Tennyson; his major terms, *bright* and *soft, flowers* and *hours,* were Tennyson's before him; but he accented their atmospheres—he found it significant, for example, that *flowers* and *hours* rhymed, the sweetest of things and the most transient;[72] upon these, he stressed and centered connections of qualities with meanings.

"Earth with an atmosphere." This was Meredith's cure, too, for the split between the real and the ideal.[73] The great poets saw no split, he said, because their spirit widened out from their material; like him they wrote things "actually observed," not "a carol in mid air."[74] He was not fond of the pathetic fallacy, as a critic of his explicitly states.[75] He found to criticize in a poem of Stevenson just this point, too, mentioning in his letter the reeds "whom you deprive of their beauty by overinforming them with your sensations."[76]

Housman is notably a repeater and simplifier of the material of poetry and thought before him; his standards rested strongly in the materials of seasonal force and life and death with which he dealt, and though he was I think an innovator too, that does not concern us here, nor his straight acceptance of a minor amount of fallacy. But Hopkins is a poet of more immediate interest, treated largely, in current writing, as if he spoke a special tongue, and speaking actually, in the range of our concern, words full of a rich contemporary convention.

---

[72] *Letters of Algernon Charles Swinburne,* ed. Gosse and Wise, Vol. I, App. I. And the description: I, letter iv.

[73] *Letters,* I, 156–157.

[74] *Ibid.,* p. 45.

[75] William Chislett, Jr., *George Meredith,* p. 213.

[76] *Letters,* I, 290.

Hopkins was a student of Ruskin; this shows through his note-books and journals, I think, more clearly than that he was a student of Pater, which was more literally true. "Ruskin, it seems to me, has the insight of a dozen critics, but intemperance and *wrongness* undoes all his good again," Hopkins wrote; he couldn't possibly be one to follow through these long Ruskinian arguments into social and moral generalization; he was a different and more precise thinker entirely. But, most fundamentally, he had a point-ing and drawing sense and a sense of the controlling structure in things; for us these are primary, and they make a primary likeness.

I venture to hope you will approve of some of the sketches in a Ruskinese point of view:—if you do not, who will, my sole congenial thinker on art?

I think I have told you that I have particular periods of admiration for particular things in Nature; for a certain time that I am astonished at the beauty of a tree, shape, effect etc. then when the passion, so to speak, has subsided, it is consigned to my treasury of explored beauty, and acknowl-edged with admiration and interest ever after, while something new takes its place in my enthusiasm. The present fury is the ash, and perhaps barley and two shapes of growth in leaves and one in tree boughs and also a conformation of fine-weather cloud.[77]

The ash, leaves, and clouds are all familiar; they are Ruskin's and Pre-Raphaelite passions, too. There is also familiar the sense of working order, organic structure, intended form of things which Ruskin marveled at and which Hopkins calls "inscape," and which he sees governing, in the new breadth of his time to which Swinburne contributed, even "the behaviour of things in slack and decay as one can see even in the pining of the skin of the old and even in a skeleton . . ."[78] Hopkins ponders Ruskin's sense of structure and event:

It is so true what Ruskin says talking of the carriage in Turner's Pass of Faido that what he could not forget was that "he had come by the road." And what is this running instress, so independent of at least the immediate scape of the thing, which unmistakeably distinguishes and individualizes things?[79]

---

[77] Gerard Manley Hopkins, *Further Letters,* ed. Claude C. Abbott, p. 55; also p. 166.
[78] *The Note-books and Papers of Gerard Manley Hopkins,* ed. Humphry House, p. 149.
[79] *Ibid.,* pp. 153–154.

Here is the way he himself looks, what he sees: an amount of detail, stress, and intensity which we have by now begun to be aware of through the poets, though never so dramatically:

> I do not think I have ever seen anything more beautiful than the bluebell I have been looking at. I know the beauty of our Lord by it. It(s inscape) is (mixed of) strength and grace, like an ash (tree). The head is strongly drawn over (backwards) and arched down like a cutwater (drawing itself back from the line of the keel). The lines of the bells strike and overlie this, rayed but not symmetrically, some lie parallel. They look steely against (the) paper, the shades lying between the bells and behind the cockled petal-ends and nursing up the precision of their distinctness, the petal-ends themselves being delicately lit.[80]

The beauty of the Lord is known not (1) by a "worthy" magnificent object or (2) by a delicate bluebell which in its very modesty and perfection speaks of the presence of God through all nature. The beauty of the Lord is known, for Hopkins and for many of his time since Tennyson, by the bluebell's arch, symmetry, steely look, precision of shade, and delicate light. It is the way Ruskin knew the Sermon on the Mount in the snowdrop: not because it was a flower—for the celandine expressly would not do,—but because of the way it was made. Always some material is apt to reveal some spirit, and, having looked long at the kinds of objects for the revelation, with content, the poets were now moved further to look within the shapes and see the signs of spirit working there.

Hopkins' theory of poetics which he wrote perhaps for Pater, and later referred to again and again, is patterned to explain and include this focus. Fundamentally, his theory of beauty is concerned with *relation,* of likes and unlikes, of wholes and parts, of words and ideas. Poetry for him, through its structure, intensifies and vivifies these relations, and uses parallelism, or comparison, with especial strength because of its structure. What things are like what other things, and to what emotional effect in com-

---

[80] *Ibid.,* pp. 133–134.

parison; how unlikes relate to likes to make a pattern; how poetry shows a sense of wholes by showing likeness where only difference had been seen; how words by their "prepossessions of emotion" and their tendency to associate themselves in a standard "poetic language," foster and establish the common recognitions of likeness—these are the concerns of Hopkins' various technical essays. The bearing of his whole theory on the use of the pathetic fallacy is simply this, implicitly: that there is not much force in it, it belongs to an old way of seeing and is valid but does not provide the vivid comparison of qualities with which poetry is intensely concerned.

Wordsworth, as one remembers, wrote a prose note to his "Lines in Early Spring" in which he described, with early devotion to pattern, the boughs in search of light, the slant of sunshine, and the color of leaves. Then he went on to tell of the feelings of the birds and flowers there, and his own feelings. Hopkins in his Journal has such a passage of description from underneath a tree. The position is almost identical, and much of the choice of detail; but there are two major differences. One is the absence of any resulting fallacy, in the prose and even in the poetry as far as Wordsworth's kind goes; and the other is the use of a major image of structural likeness which Wordsworth would have found completely irrelevant.

The hangers of small but barky branches, seen black against the leaves from within, look like ship-tackle. When you climbed to the top of the tree and came out the sky looked as if you could touch it and it was as if you were in a world made up of these three colours, the green of the leaves lit through by the sun, the blue of the sky, and the grey blaze of their upper sides against it.[81]

If, concerning Wordsworth's scene, the question "So what?" were asked, the answer of Wordsworth's poetry would be, essentially, "So the scene felt, and made me feel and ponder on man and nature"; while for Hopkins the answer would be, "So things

---

[81] *Note-books and Papers,* p. 124.

seen in the light of each other, in their quality, proportion, and relation, are beautiful, and represent the beauty of God's work." It is by reason of this change of emphasis that Hopkins could be disappointed in Wordsworth though he liked his skill and sensitivity of perception.

I must say that Wordsworth often disappoints me when I come upon a passage I knew by quotation: it seems less pointed, less excellent, with its context than without.[82]

It is the very meaning, the value, the relation, and so the nature, of the object that has changed for Hopkins and his time.

We speak of Hopkins' time, and mean the evident bond and likeness in thought of poets from Tennyson to Housman. But meanwhile what were the nonpoets, the popular critics of the time having to say about poetry and its course? Was the "new" poetry recognized for the newness we have here noted in it? Partly yes and partly no. The general critics—Horne, say, whose *New Spirit of the Age* was published in 1844 (in renewal of Hazlitt's); Arnold and Dallas, whose work was central to the 'sixties; Shairp and Selkirk and Palgrave, who wrote mainly of poetry and Nature; and Pater and Hamilton, who wrote mainly of poetry and Art—all made the usual critical complaints about poetic ideas, and looked back on various pasts with favor, but all had some recognition that there were new things to be seen in the world. Representative is the attitude toward Wordsworth.

Wordsworth was the *classic* of the 'seventies, 'eighties, 'nineties; these were his century marks in many ways. His Nature had been long accepted and looked further into; his Man was duly being revived to fit the major social interests of these decades. Those who were troubled by the obscurities of the new poets took pleasure in stressing Wordsworth's simple affections, "The few strong instincts and the few plain rules."[83] In respect to Nature, Horne,

---

[82] *Ibid.*, p. 69.
[83] Stressed by J. B. Selkirk, *Ethics and Aesthetics of Modern Poetry*, pp. 228–230.

Shairp, and Palgrave stress the fact that the eighteenth century looked at things from inside a window or on top a mountain, and that it took Wordsworth to see into the heart of things, "to make a subjectivity of his objectivity," as Horne uses the German terms.[84] Still emphasized in nature, then, was its feeling and its stimulus of feeling; and this made Hopkins feel like a Philistine, as he said.[85]

Yet, on the other hand, Selkirk who maintained the same position, criticizing modern "word-music" and the "obscurities" of Swinburne's school, as well as the "artificialities" of the eighteenth century, when he listed the "natural" beauties of nature, listed many that were new to the poetic eye, exceedingly more aesthetic than Wordsworth's, and phrased even in terms of *taste:*

> ... the taste for the poetry of Nature; the taste for the light on the hills, or the dreamy horizon line of the sea; the taste for the moon and stars, and the great tumbling clouds that, like spectral icebergs, break across them; the taste for the falling snow, the moaning wind, the setting sun; the taste for primroses in spring, the music of running water, the singing of birds, the laughter of children, and all the unwritten poetry that day unto day uttereth speech forever.[86]

Selkirk listed these beauties as being eternal, not subject to fashion, yet some of them were less than a half century in fashion when he wrote; the clouds like icebergs, particularly, were in that line of comparison by image-making which was to be called new. So the strictest traditionalists had made a certain amount of unconscious acceptance of new values in things.

As early as 1844, moreover, R. H. Horne was popularly discussing the conception of Wordsworth as prophet, and concluding that Wordsworth was "prophet of the *past*," on this basis: that he was a poet of eternal forms, while what was new was rich

---

[84] Richard Henry Horne, *A New Spirit of the Age,* pp. 178, 180, 190; and John Campbell Shairp, *On Poetic Interpretation of Nature,* and Francis Palgrave, *Landscape in Poetry.*

[85] *Note-books,* p. 81.

[86] Selkirk, *op. cit.,* pp. 102–103.

image, dreaming glory, and vague emotion."[87] So a clear line of change was laid down, which was not far from the truth, at least as poetic device reflects that truth. Hunt, Browning, and very notably Tennyson, Horne held to be new poets in 1844. Influence of Keats and Shelley was to be seen in Tennyson, and Tennyson's own characteristics were his precision of outline, as in "The Kraken," and his dreaming toward the unknown, which Horne felt to be poetry's essential.[88]

As the shift in interest and technique was taking place, then, it was at least partially noticed by popular critics. Horne did indeed have a discerning perception to work from, and that was Hazlitt's. Some years before, in discussing Schlegel's theory of romanticism and classicism, Hazlitt had made, as the distinction between the two attitudes, the distinction between objects important for their own sakes and objects important by association.[89] Now by Hazlitt's own perspective, these meant objects unified and majestic in themselves, like Greek temples, as distinguished from objects arousing personal feelings by association with emotion, such as Gothic buildings. Both were important to Wordsworth, though his stress was on "eternal," since some associations of feeling were most eternal of all; and the distinction did not apply to the new Victorian view. But the point is that such a view of the kinds of importance an object could have, apart from the psychology of beauty and sublimity, gave Horne a basis for his perceptive distinction between pre-1840 and post-1840.

A critic who had very little idea about what "the object as in itself it really is"[90] really could mean was Arnold. The phrase was a favorite of his, but it was so surrounded by social theory that,

---

[87] Horne, *op. cit.*, p. 190.
[88] *Ibid.*, pp. 193–194, 360 ff.
[89] Frederick E. Pierce, *Currents and Eddies in the English Romantic Generation*, p. 290.
[90] Arnold, "The Function of Criticism," 1864; and Lionel Trilling, *Matthew Arnold*, Introductory Note, p. xii: "*To see the object as it really is* was the essence of Arnold's teaching; . . . " See for use of phrase "thing in itself," Edward Taube, "German Influence on English Vocabulary of the Nineteenth Century," *Jour. English and Germanic Philol.*, XXXIX (1940), pp. 486–493.

as far as I can see, it never had a chance to unfold its implications for Arnold. What he opposed it to was "practical consequence"; he was deeply in earnest about seeing things and works of art as wholes, rather than in partial effects, but he had little vivid sense of the facts the wholes might be comprised of. He wanted interpretation rather than images; he was essentially a Wordsworthian in his aesthetics. Partly, he was puzzled; he asked,

> ... is there an object which inevitably calls forth our emotion, or does the emotion of the subjective observer give significance to, create, the object? Is the world self-sustaining or is it sustained by the experience of man?[91]

Yet he defended the poetic value of the pathetic fallacy with vigor.

> The mighty world of eye and ear also yields moral meaning, it also demands the pathetic fallacy, though more legitimately, for in this connection the eye and ear are dominant, the critical mind is in abeyance and whatever morality is found is based avowedly on the subjective insight of the moment's mood.[92]

In aesthetics E. S. Dallas seems to me a less accepting and accepted, but a wiser man. Writing in Arnold's decade of the 'sixties, and himself praising Arnold justly for his turn away from rhetoric toward social setting, and himself, too, stressing the "whole-making" power of the imagination which Coleridge had so well established, Dallas presented a much less limited defense for the fallacy by putting it in its place as a *kind,* rather than a *degree,* of art. This establishment of kinds of vision he makes in terms of a philosophy of comparison much like Hopkins', and related to Coleridge; a psychology of the "play of thought" toward pleasure, unconscious and whole-making, seeing likes, making comparisons, creating images as symbols of the comparisons, and so creating wholes. The tendency of the mind to similitude has three phases: the dramatic or sympathetic, which says, "I am that or like that"; the lyric or egotistic, which

---

[91] Trilling, *Matthew Arnold*, p. 92.
[92] *Ibid.,* p. 91.

says, "That is I or like me"; and the epic or objective, which says, "That is that or like that." Of the second, Dallas says,

Mr. Ruskin calls this form of imagery the pathetic fallacy, and says that it is only the second order of poets who much delight in it—seldom the first order. But this is surely a mistake. It by no means denotes the height of art—first-rate, second-rate, or tenth-rate; it denotes the kind of art—it belongs to the lyrical mood.[93]

Now the fact that ways of looking at the world are being listed as alternatives, and that comparison is basic to these ways as far as poetry is concerned, is an important fact for poetry as for philosophy. It takes the place of the old sublime–beautiful opposition which Coleridge solved—satisfactorily to himself, evidently—partly in terms of comparison. Dallas in mid-century managed what Arnold failed to manage for aesthetics: a view which included both the old world of Wordsworth and the new world (which *had* been born) of Tennyson, the Pre-Raphaelites, Hopkins, as alternative choices and ways of sight. The form, which included the pathetic fallacy, of saying that nature is like man is acceptable as poetic; the form saying that one object is like another is poetic, too. Dallas has further a good deal of importance to say historically of the relation of men to nature in the flower-pressing and -sketching period of the nineteenth century; his whole work surveys the century from its middle with startlingly distinct perspective. But what is of central importance to us is that this one critic gave at once to Wordsworth's method, and to Hopkins', theoretical justification and poetic value, even though his own heart was closer to the one method than the other. On the new basis of thought Ruskin had set up a subordination, which Dallas more rationally made an alternative.

Now to take up, in summary, the alternative, "That is like that." We have been pursuing its early and meager implications through this study, and they come together under Dallas' phrase,

[93] Eneas Dallas, *The Gay Science*, p. 282.

still small in comparison with what they will grow to be. The nineteenth-century form of objectivity ("epic," as Dallas called it, thinking of an older kind of objectivity), of object "for its own sake," "in itself as it really is," is by no means object isolated from wider implications of spirit, feeling, and God, but rather object indicating those relations partly through its own qualities and structure rather than by direct association with man. Shape, color, texture, odor, inner form—these terms as they became of greater and greater importance to poetry put the emphasis more and more on "That is like that," since likeness could so strengthen and support the impressions of sense. We have seen how these words of sense discrimination grew stronger in plain prose description between Wordsworth's and Ruskin's time; how they became more involved in critical discussion; and how, at the other extreme, they were to be seen entering even into the close traditional device of the pathetic fallacy, altering it as they diminished it.

Here we watch, in other words, the growth of a major material in poetry and thought: the material of sensed quality. It has thus been visible precisely because closely examined in the small range of a single device, and then looked for in wider thought only as that bore directly upon the range of the device. We have seen *sweet, soft, dim, gold* come between the object and its associated feeling by reason of an assumption that the foundation of feeling was in quality rather than in object—an assumption destroying the old fixed associations and creating new ones in terms of sense perception. This, in Baumgarten's original use of the word in the eighteenth century, is *aesthetic,* the stress of sense perception. This too, and still, was what the 1890's meant by aesthetics and art for art's sake: not the lack of relation to spirit, but the direct relation to spirit, of the qualities which men could perceive by sight, smell, taste, hearing, touch. By their time, indeed, they had got only a little way with the idea; the problems of significance in temperature and texture and the turning over of a leaf are still going on, in spite even of all the Imagist contributions. What was spoken of in derogation of the Imagists, their intense pleasure in the discovery of likeness between two sense impressions, is just the pleasure which Dallas and Hopkins wrote of as important to poetry, and just the poetic material which has been growing firmly all through the century since Tennyson, or more faintly since Burns, Shelley, and Keats.

Along with the decrease of stated feeling and fallacy, and the increase or change of objects most carefully considered, the richening in reference of many nouns, there grew up the importance of the adjective of quality, the *bright, dim,* and *sweet* which made the new bonds of connection between feeling and object. We have seen how they prospered for Shelley, Keats, and the Pre-Raphaelites. It is surprising to me, but true, that this very growth of a new poetic material as we have observed it is visible in the simplest primary listings of the Concordances. Let us look at twelve of these, from Pope to Housman,[94] and count the words most used in each one, omitting common auxiliaries and pronouns and counting all forms of a word as one. The results reveal a pattern of thought like this: *Man,* his *life* and his *love* are primary for most. There are major verbs such as *see* and *make,* and the adjective *good*. There are specifications, from Gray on, of *eye* and *hand,* and of *heart* and *thought, death, spirit, God,* and *truth* for many. Now all these words are man's; they belong to him in spirit or body. All of Pope's, Cowper's, Coleridge's, Browning's main words are of this kind, and for all the poets, indeed, the words of quality somewhat outward or apart are many fewer. Yet for Collins, first of all, three main words are *fair, sweet,* and *wild;* for Burns, *dear, sweet,* and *day;* for Wordsworth, *day* and *time;* for Keats, *sweet* and *fair;* for Shelley, *light* and *earth;* for Tennyson, *day, great, light, sweet;* for Housman, *day* and *night.*

---

[94] See Bibliography for concordance list.

Here are the adjectives dawning on the scene of poetry in a truly visible dawn. It is a dawn, too, visible even in the narrow reaches of the pathetic fallacy, as we have seen for all but Burns and Collins. The major new poetic words are words of sensed quality as well as emotion: sweetness and light being, too, by a remarkable consistency, the qualities of culture for which Arnold speaks in *Culture and Anarchy,* though he consciously derived the terms from a metaphor of Swift's. Such is the power of the new adjective in nineteenth-century thought that it is taken to name an ideal, as well as a quality, and is put down by many poets far more often than most other words in the language. It has become a prime poetic material.

Now it is against this very material, in its effect, that modern critical objection is raised. Our total picture of nineteenth-century poetic language is of a language blurred, too widely connotative, weakened and diluted by adjectival modification. What seems to me a due and deep discrimination in its own time is now held to be a dilution by ours. How are these two positions to be reconciled? Mainly, I think, by a much closer knowledge than we have as yet. Consider, for example, just a little of the modern critical attitude in contrast or in comparison to the attitude which we have been surveying in one of its minor forms. Cleanth Brooks, John Crowe Ransom, Allen Tate, William Empson, Frederick Bateson all make the same criticism of the "romantic" language of the nineteenth century. Its technique was "evasive" and "dissolving."[95] It had lost, in the eighteenth century, its "organic suggestiveness," and exploited instead its vague dream qualities.[96] There was a loosening of connection between denotation and connotation, a working at the extreme of intention in language, giving denotation over to science and keeping "a continually thinning flux of peripheral connotations."[97] There was the tend-

---

[95] William Empson, *Seven Types of Ambiguity,* pp. 222, 242.
[96] F. W. Bateson, *English Poetry and the English Language,* p. 94 ff.
[97] Allen Tate, *Reason in Madness,* p. 71.

ency for splendors to cut loose from ideas.[98] There was the aim, in which Romanticism and Symbolism were allied, of generating shadowy imprecise moods as opposed to sharply realized meanings, the use of vague and blurred as opposed to sharp and detailed.[99] There was the "Romantic lack of interest in the object," the expression of feeling and mood and the consequent mistreatment of objects as ornaments or illustrations.[100] There was the Romantic confusion with music and revery, the "harmonics of the note."[101] There was Arthur Symons' metaphor for the nineteenth-century imagination as a "soft, not quite transparent, veil of mist, like the down on fruit," over a line of bare trees.[102] Finally, there was a whole complex connection between the Romantics, particularly the Pre-Raphaelites, and the French Symbolistes, involving, too, the America of the 1830's through Poe, who was Tennyson's devotee by 1843, who is said in his "Heresy of the Didactic" to have founded *la poésie pure,* and who wrote significantly that "we can, at any time, double the true beauty of an actual landscape by half-closing our eyes as we look at it."[103]

Characteristic nineteenth-century vision and consequent diction amounts, in other words, to a large slice of poetic problem, and it has currently been too largely treated to achieve much correlation between fact and interpretation. Certainly critical consensus, as summarized here so rashly and briefly, provides a consistent view of the situation; but it is, I think, a view built up strongly as an opposition to that which modern poetry would build for itself. The basic contrast between nineteenth-century diffusion and modern fusion is perhaps more flattering to the latter than descriptive of either. At least this generalization may be made: that the modern critical view of nineteenth-century

---

[98] John Livingston Lowes, *Convention and Revolt in Poetry*, p. 219.
[99] Cleanth Brooks, *Modern Poetry and the Tradition*, pp. 54–59.
[100] John Crowe Ransom, *The World's Body*, pp. 111–112, 144–145, 231–232.
[101] Charles Baudouin, *Contemporary Studies*, trans. Eden and Cedar Paul, pp. 203 ff.
[102] Arthur Symons, *The Romantic Movement in English Poetry*, p. 14.
[103] Poe, *Marginalia*, quoted by Van der Vat, *The Fabulous Opera*, p. 149.

poetics seems on the one hand to disdain a phase which we have noticed constantly and intently aimed at by the poets, and, on the other, quite to ignore the opposite face of that phase, the growth of sharp, detailed, and specific discriminations in language and vision. On the one hand, the Romantics were perfectly conscious of their stress on "cloud," and approved its significance; on the other, they were working toward the poetizing of more sharp fact of sense perception than there had been in their world before. Their language, as we have seen it here, seems, in other words, not to have been languishing in a realm rarefied away from fact, but rather to have been making poetic sense of the progressively new interests of the human mind.

We may recall, then, by way of summary in terms of modern emphasis, these two aspects of language and interest as they have made themselves plain through the device of the pathetic fallacy and its surrounding view. First, the matter of cloud and mist and blurring toward infinity: in these terms a recent survey of Romanticism (printed in the *Publications of the Modern Language Association* in 1940) essentializes the Romantic mind; yet so did John Foster in 1805, calling it

. . . like a hemisphere of cloud scenery, filled with an ever-moving train of changing, melting forms, of every color, mingled with rainbows, meteors, and an occasional gleam of pure sunlight, all vanishing away, the mental like this natural imagery, when its hour is up, without leaving anything behind but the wish to recover the vision.[104]

And so, still, in 1856, Ruskin was writing of the current stress:

And we find that whereas all the pleasure of the mediaeval was in *stability, definiteness,* and *luminosity,* we are expected to rejoice in darkness, and triumph in mutability; to lay the foundation of happiness in things which momentarily change or fade; and to expect the utmost satisfaction and instruction from what it is impossible to arrest, and difficult to comprehend. . . . So that, if a general and characteristic name were needed for modern landscape art, none better could be invented than "the service of clouds."[105]

---

[104] Pierce, *op. cit.*, pp. 288–289.
[105] *Modern Painters,* Vol. III, Pt. IV, chap. xvi, §§1, 2.

The trait was noted by most writers through the century, as with especial vividness by Arnold in his description of "Celtic" characteristics.

But under the mists, according to Symons' metaphor, of Romantic imagination, was the line of bare trees. Beneath the blur and vague infinity-reaching were recognized structures of nature, not merely in direct visualized aspect but in perceived inner form of stem and branch. This dual working of precise and vague, the one to balance and enforce the other into a total view, was also recognized in its time, even by "a working cork-cutter in Sunderland," Thomas Dixon, who wrote to Rossetti in 1859:

I desired to read some of the *Germ,* and then tell you how much I liked them, or otherwise. . . . Why is it for [*sic*] these pictures and essays . . . , being so realistic, yet produce on the mind such a vague and dreamy sensation, approaching as it were the Mystic Land of a Bygone Age? . . . There is [in] them the life which I long for, and which to me never seems realizable in this life.[106]

Why did snowdrop speak of Sermon on the Mount, and bluebell of the Lord, and girl's song of old unhappy far-off things, and all, even Wilde's own sunflower, of "underlying truths"? Why did the concrete and the vague go so closely together? It was not, on the whole, for the nineteenth century, a matter of symbolizing of the inexpressible by a conventionalized expressible, in the manner of standard symbolizing. It was, I surmise— and certainly we must know much more about the psychology of sight at that time,—fundamentally an increasingly precise way of seeing natural objects, and hence an increasingly uncertain and nebulous way of interpreting the large amount of new detail acquired. The progress of vision in the past two centuries has been a progress toward closer and closer discrimination of quality; the progress of interpretation has therefore been away from strict association with objects as representative, and away from response in the large terms of universalized emotion, toward the meanings

---

[106] *Ruskin: Rossetti: Preraphaelitism,* p. 221.

and significances of sense perception of qualities. Therefore, as we have noted, the interchange and blending of sense values have become of increasing importance to poetry, as likewise the whole relation of minor impressions to involuntary memory which was of interest to Rossetti and Harland, as to Proust; and so likewise the comparing of two quality perceptions, on which so many theories of beauty, including those of Coleridge, Dallas, and Hopkins, were based, and which centered its vocabulary in the names of colors, textures, temperatures, and in the adjective.

This adjective of the nineteenth century, this *sweet, dim, cool, blue, silver, bright,* of Keats and Shelley, of Tennyson and the Pre-Raphaelites, and individually of Hopkins, and eventually in the renewed insistence of the Imagists: is it after all a blurring force in poetic language? For modern poets who have found the vividness of two objects in the implied comparison of a metaphysical root-metaphor to be direct in impact, yes, the adjective as standard of comparison seems an unnecessary and diluting intermediate. But it must be remembered that moderns have now in mind so that it may be implied, all the full qualitative force which for the nineteenth century had still to be stated to be understood. John Donne's and George Herbert's objects were bare of much that we see in them because we are looking through the nineteenth century, the excesses of which we malign. Horne called Robert Browning in 1844 "the Columbus of an impossible discovery";[107] and in truth Browning's contemporaries, too, were engaged in discoveries more or less possible, now pretty much assumed by us as easy. We make "condensation" our watchword in opposition to what we think of as diffuseness; but it is important that condensation was equally the watchword of Tennyson, of Hopkins, of Rossetti, of Meredith.[108] It was just the adjective,

---

[107] Horne, *op. cit.,* p. 296.
[108] For examples of stress on condensation see: Tennyson, *Memoir,* p. 166; Ruskin's praise of Browning in De Vane, *Browning Handbook,* pp. 151–152; Ruskin, *Praeterita,* p. 123; Hopkins, *Note-books,* "On the Origin of Beauty," pp. 82 ff.

too, which made the condensation for them, which held in itself the core of significant likenesses central to poetic thought. Ruskin has a footnote which says fully what I have been trying to say. He is listing notable things—"bright silver moss—glossy gray stems of the cherry trees—here and there a chestnut—sharp, soft, and starry . . . " and his footnote to *starry* is,

I meant—the leaves themselves, sharp, the clustered nuts, soft, the arrangement of leaves, starry.[100]

This is, in a few lines, the detail of perception, the focus of interest, and the problem and solution of statement with which nineteenth-century poetry was intensely concerned. The use of language, though adjectival, is not vague, diffuse, connotative, or marginal, in terms of its own purposes; the adjective provides a legitimate alternative to metaphoric comparison; the prime words, saying the most in least, are the words of quality.

A century ago, then, one kind of poetic condensation and focus gave way in perceptible degree to another. The enduring interest in stating the unknown in terms of the known made a main shift of its terms from object and emotion to quality and sense perception, working inward from outline to detail, as men discerned more, and as more words became available to poetry by use. The pathetic fallacy stated a great likeness between man and nature in terms of aspects and of sympathies of feeling; then clearly in one decade it lessened and altered in its significance for poets, as the alternative power of qualitative comparison between object and object in terms of senses made itself felt. Though the change from one means of sight and expression to the other was gradual in part, it was nevertheless particularly clear in a few poets who believed together; and it was a major change. It was part of that new world which Arnold felt not yet born, yet which had been born indeed, and in which we live and write.

---

[100] *Praeterita*, II, 365. See Hopkins' *Note-books*, p. 108, for another "inscape" of chestnuts.

IV. CONCLUSION

No SINGLE item provides a better natural summary of the course of the object through bestowed emotion in the nineteenth century than the career of Wordsworth's primrose. This small flower took to itself all the main stresses of thought: first the emphasis on aspect, which made it so minor; then the connection with deep feelings which Peter Bell so ruthlessly missed; then interpretation by Dallas as "representative fact," which was so true to Wordsworth's own position; then emphasis on color, shape, and quality, by Ruskin and Hopkins; then finally, complaint by the modern "pure poetry" school, that the flower should ever have had a soul imposed upon it. The primrose grew from a sharer in God's sympathy to an "instress of brilliancy, sort of starriness," and that growth is at the exact center of the decline and fall of the pathetic fallacy. The device followed and expressed, and in turn perhaps led, the vision.

We may look in chronological order at the major statements about the primrose, that flower which the Oxford Dictionary defines as "a well-known plant bearing pale yellowish flowers in early spring, growing wild in woods and hedges and on banks, especially in clayey soil, and cultivated in many varieties as a garden plant." First, most notable, and of great effect was Wordsworth's statement, in the describing of Peter Bell's hardheartedness, that

A primrose by the river's brim
A yellow primrose was to him,
And it was nothing more.

Small change it made on Peter's heart . . .

In vain, through water, earth, and air,
The soul of happy sound was spread . . .

This situation touched the hearts of hundreds and opened their eyes to the possible import of their observations. By 1826 Miss

Mitford was able to boast a deeper sight than Peter's and to say, "primrosy is the epithet which this year will retain in my recollection."[1] People went walking to see the primrose and bestow their feelings upon it, and to feel in it the spirit of the universe. This attitude E. S. Dallas in 1866 explained and exalted, treating it with due perspective as one of the types of poetry and vision, widening Wordsworth's meaning justly, yet flexibly enough to include much of the meaning that was still to come, using, as we have, the lines from "Peter Bell" as significant.

Now let us ask what is it that the man of imagination, the man of thought, sees more than Peter Bell in a primrose? He sees in it a type. It is not merely a fact; it is a representative fact. The primrose by the river's brim stands for all primroses—and more, for all flowers—and yet more, for all life. It comes to signify more than itself. By itself it is but a single atom of existence. Our thought sees in it the entirety of existence and raises it into a mighty whole. This is what I mean by the whole of intension, which predominates in lyrical art, and in arts not lyrical when they rise in the early or lyrical period of a nation's life. The units of existence are intensified and exalted into things of universal existence.[2]

The emphasis here on intention, the inward force toward universality, is not foreign to Wordsworth, and the whole explanation is sympathetic to him, yet it leads, too, toward some justification of Ruskin's stress on inward workings of objects. Wordsworth and Ruskin, whom we have seen to be literally far apart, are thus brought theoretically closer by this mediator of the 'sixties.

Ruskin's own statement on the ways of looking at a primrose testifies both to the tolerance and perspective which Dallas also displays, the allowance for alternatives, and the honest newness of Ruskin's phrasing:

So, then, we have the three ranks: the man who perceives rightly, because he does not feel, and to whom the primrose is very accurately the primrose, because he does not love it. Then, secondly, the man who perceives wrongly,

---

[1] *New English Dictionary.*
[2] Eneas Dallas, *The Gay Science,* pp. 292–293.

because he feels, and to whom the primrose is anything else than a primrose: a star, or a sun, or a fairy's shield, or a forsaken maiden. And then, lastly, there is the man who perceives rightly in spite of his feelings, and to whom the primrose is for ever nothing else than itself—a little flower, apprehended in the very plain and leafy fact of it, whatever and how many soever the associations and passions may be that crowd around it.[3]

"The very plain and leafy fact of it" is the fact of that revolution in poetry and thought of which we have been speaking. The phrase is one as memorable for the nineteenth century as Shelley's "shape, and hue, and odour, and sweet sound," Swinburne's "all form, all sound, all colour, and all thought," Browning's "shapes of things, their colours, lights, and shades," and they all direct a critical attention to their main line of sensed poetic material. The physical world was new, they make clear, and new before Darwin.

Hopkins, too, was Ruskin's poet in close perception. He, not only for bluebell and chestnut, but specifically for primrose, speaks of "the plain and leafy fact of it":

Take a *few* primroses in a glass and the instress of—brilliancy, sort of starriness: I have not the right word—so simple a flower gives is remarkable. It is, I think, due to the strong swell given by the deeper yellow middle.[4]

With these three men, with Ruskin, Dallas, Hopkins, we have seen set, I think, the grounds for a main new poetic material. We have, further, the toleration for other ways which was to fade when "Imagism" came to be revived as a program. In his introduction to his *Anthology of Pure Poetry* in 1924, George Moore belligerently sets up the mid-century mark again, but now with scorn of the Wordsworthian device. This is still a modern version of the primrose problem:

So perhaps the time has come for somebody to ask if there is not more poetry in things than in ideas, and more pleasure in Gautier's *Tulipe* than in Wordsworth's ecclesiastical, political, and admonitory sonnets. My father used to admire the sonnet on Westminster Bridge, and I admired it until

---

[3] *Modern Painters*, Vol. III, Pt. IV, chap. xii, §8.
[4] Hopkins' *Note-books*, pp. 142–143.

I could no longer escape from the suspicion that it was not the beautiful image of a city overhanging a river at dawn that detained the poet, but the hope that he might once more discern a soul in nature. Having, I said to myself, discerned a soul in a primrose by a river's brim, it would seem to him parsimonious to limit the habitation of the soul to a woodland flower, and he would soon begin to seek it in bricks and mortar.[5]

That the primrose could run such a gamut of observation in one century; that Peter Bell's single flower could be chosen for feeling, generalized into type, denounced for soul, while in the meantime its *instress* and its *leafy fact* were growing clear to view, is in itself a small epic of changing event which tells, too, the story of the pathetic fallacy. By 1884 there was even a "Primrose League," for British Conservatives; Disraeli and fellow gentlemen were discriminating enough to see more in the primrose than in any other flower, and the *Westminster Gazette* could comment in 1897, "Primrosery is not so much a reasoned faith as a social cult."[6] So the modest sympathies of the flower were reaching every heart in one way or another, while the poets and philosophers had gone on to other qualities of its nature and were perceiving it in other terms. The primrose: the feeling flower: the leafy fact. One phase must not be remembered without the other for the nineteenth century.

We have been concerned in this study with the poetic use of a device during two hundred years. We have seen that at a definite point the pathetic fallacy lessened in amount and changed in quality, and we have looked at the nature of that change and its consequences for our time. We have been concerned with problems of continuity, change, direction, assimilation, articulation, sources of thought, individual consciousness and response, accumulated contribution, and present recognition, all through one small kind of combination of object and emotion. In these terms it is possible to state some facts in sum, as follows.

[5] *Anthology of Pure Poetry*, pp. 19–20.
[6] *New English Dictionary*.

That poets, major and minor, tended to agree, over an extended period, however different their styles and contributions, in the amount and character of the convention employed.

That in one poet a major change in the device was suddenly visible, and thenceforward sustained, but that small signs of the change were visible beforehand, once one had been directed to them by the acceptances of the one major poet of change.

That an almost steady downward line of quantity and quality in the device can be traced through the century, the minor poets perhaps taking the change more slowly than the major. About this relationship much more should be known.

That the device in its decline did not retain all its conventional forms, but tended to merge, blend, and take in some of the very new material which, by its new power in thought, was driving out the old device.

That the course of articulation of the controlling thought seems to be this: from incidental noting of new things and significances, with prose comments not lived up to in verse (Wordsworth's prose notes); to hints in criticism and verse (Scott, Shelley); to a full new use in verse without an as yet sustaining critical consciousness (Tennyson); to a period of full critical, poetic, and artistic interworking (the Pre-Raphaelites); to further original assumption and elucidation (Hopkins); to decline in interest on the one hand (the metaphysical revival), and to a revival in a conscious sense of something suddenly new and clear (the Imagists).

That the source of power for the thought seems to have been a plainly developing literal vision, an increase along one line of concentration, which then led to both scientific discovery and philosophical synthesis as well as poetical and critical statement. Darwin, for example, though he might well have been thought the one to influence the pathetic fallacy's decline, was merely part of the time and group through which it declined. For Darwin, as for Tennyson, the preceding directing hints had been many, and his work too was part of a cumulation; it was not a directing force for a device in poetry even so closely connected with it as this one. So far as I know, no unified intellectual statement established Tennyson's new material, but rather a widespread interest moving in a direction in which his individual vagary of minute perception also moved.

That the *newness* was not unconsciously absorbed, after being phrased by Tennyson, but was consciously hailed and recognized even in the sound of the language, and was followed unerringly.

That the relation of the device to individual poets illuminates problems of their work. The fact that Wordsworth, for example, began seeing variety in nature which he omitted to put in poetry, fearing the "tyranny of the eye" in its old sense of outward aspect, explains much of the conflict in his mind between literal and idealizing observation, and indicates what new justifications for detail it would be necessary for Ruskin to make. The fact that Tennyson had no conscious aesthetic theory for the new aesthetics which he practiced prevented him from making its force sustaining in his poetry, as even the small details of the fallacy in "In Memoriam" reflect. The fact that Hopkins' aesthetic theory and use of device both were an active participation in the theory and practice of his time suggests how solidly his originality was fixed in contemporaneity and active convention.

That our criticism of Romanticism today, often in terms of poetic language, ignores the continuity of its growth from earlier stages: its contribution of qualitative perception and consequent adjectival stress, the power of the adjective in poetic condensation; the relation of dimness not only to the earlier "sublime" but to the modern psychology of the subconscious, the interaction of senses, and the force of memory.

That we need much more knowledge not only of the deeper reaches of this device—into the pre-1740's, into minor poetry, into other work of the writers here considered, into our own immediate present,—but more knowledge also of all the other devices, attitudes, expressions, words of poetry, as they condense and enforce by pattern the general expression of the times. The life of thought has its material and its objectivity in these terms, and still we are able as yet to recognize little of their contexts and continuities.

APPENDIX

TABLE OF FREQUENCIES

AMOUNT OF PATHETIC FALLACY IN THE WORK OF TWENTY-FOUR POETS
(See text, pp. 190–191, for explanation; see Bibliography,
pp. 299–300, for works indicated.)

Poet	Pathetic fallacy in number of lines	Average number of lines in which one pathetic fallacy occurs
Collins	30/1550	52
Gray	20/1100	55
Beattie	20/1100	55
Cowper	100/5200	52
Burns	50/2000	40
Darwin	80/2450	31
Blake	50/1000	20
Wordsworth	80/4900	61
Scott	25/3000	120
Byron	15/950	63
Shelley	60/3170	53
Keats	75/3470	46
	Average	54
Tennyson	130/11,100	85
Browning	10/2880	288
Rossetti	40/4570	114
Morris	35/3670	105
Swinburne	25/1540	62
Hopkins	10/1350	135
Meredith	23/2300	100
Housman	10/1350	135
Imagist Poets	20/1200	60
Pure Poetry	60/2000	33
Poetry (the magazine)	7/660	94
Eliot	5/1370	274
	Average	124

BIBLIOGRAPHY

BIBLIOGRAPHY

Editions of Poetry
(In chronological order)

William Collins. Poems, 1742–1749.
> *The Poems of Gray and Collins,* ed. Austin Lane Poole and Christopher Stone (2d ed., revised; London, Oxford Univ. Press, 1926).

Thomas Gray. Poems (not fragments), pub. 1768, and posthumous edition named above.

James Beattie, "The Minstrel," 1771–1774.
> *Elegant Extracts . . . from the Most Eminent Poets* (London: John Sharpe, *ca.* 1820), Vol. XII.

William Cowper, "The Task," 1785.
> *Poetical Works,* ed. H. S. Milford (4th ed.; London, Oxford Univ. Press, 1934).

Robert Burns, "Scottish Poems," 1786, 1787. First 2000 lines.
> *The Works of the British Poets,* ed. Thomas Park (London, 1805–1808), Vol. XXIV.

William Blake, "Songs of Innocence," 1789; "Songs of Experience," 1794.
> *Poems* (New York, Modern Library, 1930).

Erasmus Darwin, *The Botanic Garden,* Pt. I, "The Economy of Vegetation," 1789 (London, 1791).

William Wordsworth, "Lyrical Ballads," 1800.
> *Complete Poetical Works,* ed. A. J. George (Boston, Houghton, Mifflin, 1904).

Walter Scott, "The Lay of the Last Minstrel," 1805.
> *Poetical Works* (New York, Appleton, 1852).

George Gordon, Lord Byron, "Childe Harold's Pilgrimage," Canto I, 1812.
> *Complete Poetical Works* (Globe Edition; New York, Macmillan, 1927).

John Keats, *Poems,* published 1817, 1820.

Percy Bysshe Shelley, five poems, 1815–1822 ("Alastor," "Peter Bell the Third," "Epipsychidion," "Adonais," "The Triumph of Life").
> *Complete Poetical Works of John Keats and Percy Bysshe Shelley* (New York, Modern Library, 1932).

Alfred, Lord Tennyson, six groups of poems, 1830–1890 ("Juvenilia," "Lady of Shalott and Other Poems," "Morte d'Arthur," "In Memoriam," "Maud," "Demeter and Other Poems").
> *Poems and Plays* (New York, Modern Library, 1938).

Robert Browning, "Men and Women," 1855.
> As selected in *Poems and Plays* (New York, Modern Library, 1934).

Dante Gabriel Rossetti, "Poems," and "Songs and Sonnets," 1840–1870.
> *Poems and Translations* (Everyman's Library; London, Dent, 1912).

William Morris, *Defence of Guenevere and Other Poems,* 1858 (London, Bell and Daldy, 1858).

Algernon Charles Swinburne, *Poems and Ballads,* Second Series, 1878 (London, Chatto and Windus, 1878). First 1500 lines.

Gerard Manley Hopkins, *Poems,* 1876–1889.
> *Poems,* ed. Robert Bridges (2d ed.; London, Oxford Univ. Press, 1930).

George Meredith, *Ballads and Poems of Tragic Life,* 1887 (London: Macmillan, 1887).

A. E. Housman, *A Shropshire Lad,* 1896 (London, Paul, 1896).

T. S. Eliot, *Collected Poems, 1909–1935* (New York, Harcourt, Brace, 1936). Used: 1909–1925.

Some Imagist Poets: An Anthology (Boston, Houghton, Mifflin, 1915).

Pure Poetry, ed. George Moore, 1924 (New York, Boni and Liveright, 1925). Blake to Swinburne.

Poetry, A Magazine of Verse, ed. George Dillon, Vol. LV, No. 6 (March, 1940).

CONCORDANCES

A Concordance to the Works of Alexander Pope, ed. Edwin Abbott (London, 1875).

A Concordance of the Poetical Works of William Collins, ed. Bradford Booth and Claude E. Jones (Berkeley, Univ. of Calif. Press, 1939).

A Concordance to the English Poems of Thomas Gray, ed. Alfred S. Cook (Boston, 1908).

A Complete Word and Phrase Concordance to the Poems and Songs of Robert Burns, ed. J. B. Reid (Glasgow, 1889).

A Concordance to the Poetical Works of William Cowper, ed. John Neve (London, 1887).

A Concordance to the Poetry of Samuel Taylor Coleridge, ed. Sister Eugenia Logan (St.-Mary-of-the-Woods, Ind., 1940).

A Concordance to the Poems of William Wordsworth, ed. Alfred Lane Cooper (London, 1911).

A Concordance to the Poems of John Keats, ed. D. L. Baldwin *et al.* (Carnegie Institute of Washington, 1917).

A Lexical Concordance to the Poetical Works of Percy Bysshe Shelley, ed. F. S. Ellis (London, 1892).

A Concordance to the Poetical and Dramatic Works of Alfred Lord Tennyson, ed. Arthur E. Baker (London, Paul, Trench, Trübner, 1914).

A Concordance to the Poems of Robert Browning, ed. Leslie N. Broughton and Benjamin F. Stelter (New York, 1924–1925). 2 vols.

A Concordance to the Poems of A. E. Housman, ed. Clyde K. Hyder (Lawrence, Kas., 1940).

PRIMARY CRITICISM AND THEORY

(In chronological order)

Henry Home, Lord Kames, *Elements of Criticism,* 1762 (New York, 1830). One vol., with index.

Archibald Alison, *Essays on the Nature and Principles of Taste,* 1790 (6th ed.; Edinburgh, 1825). 2 vols.

Erasmus Darwin, Interludes in *The Botanic Garden* (London, 1791).

Samuel Taylor Coleridge, *Biographia Literaria,* 1817 (Modern Readers' Series; Macmillan, 1926).

William Wordsworth, prose prefaces, etc. *Complete Poetical Works,* ed. A. J. George (Cambridge Edition; Boston, Houghton, Mifflin, 1904).

——, letters, ed. Ernest de Selincourt (Oxford, Clarendon Press).

Early Letters of William and Dorothy Wordsworth, 1787–1805 (1935).

Letters: The Middle Years, 1806–1820 (1937). 2 vols.

Letters: The Later Years, 1821–1850 (1939). 3 vols.

A Cabinet of Gems: Short Stories from the English Annuals, ed. Bradford Allen Booth (Berkeley, Univ. of Calif. Press, 1938).

Percy Bysshe Shelley, *Peacock's Memoirs of Shelley, with Shelley's Letters to Peacock,* ed. H. F. B. Brett-Smith (London, Frowde, 1909).

John Keats, *Letters,* ed. Maurice Buxton Forman (London, Oxford Univ. Press, 1931). 2 vols.

William Hazlitt, "The Spirit of the Age," in *Complete Works*, ed. P. P. Howe (21 vols.; London, Dent, 1930–1934), Vol. XI.

Richard Henry Horne, *A New Spirit of the Age* (2d ed.; London, Smith, Elder, 1844). 2 vols.

Alfred Lord Tennyson: A Memoir, by His Son [Hallam] (London, Macmillan, 1897).

Robert Browning and Elizabeth Barrett Browning, *Letters, 1845–1846* (New York, Harpers, 1899). 2 vols.

John Ruskin, *Works*, ed. E. T. Cook and Alexander Wedderburn (New York, Longmans, Green, 1903–1912). 39 vols.

———, *Praeterita* (Cabinet Edition; Boston, n.d.), 2 vols.

Ruskin as Literary Critic: Selections, ed. A. H. R. Ball (Cambridge Univ. Press, 1928).

Ruskin: Rossetti: Preraphaelitism. Papers, 1854–1862, ed. William Michael Rossetti (New York, Dodd, Mead, 1899).

Dante Gabriel Rossetti: His Family Letters, ed. William Michael Rossetti (London, 1895). 2 vols.

William Morris, *Collected Works*, with introductions by his daughter May Morris (24 vols.; New York, Longmans, Green, 1910–1915), esp. Vols. II, XXII.

Algernon Charles Swinburne, *Letters*, ed. Edmund Gosse and Thomas James Wise (New York, John Lane, 1919). 2 vols.

George Meredith, *Letters*, ed. by His Son (New York: Scribner's, 1912). 2 vols.

Gerard Manley Hopkins, *Note-books and Papers*, ed. Humphry House (London, Oxford Univ. Press, 1937).

———, *Further Letters*, ed. Claude C. Abbott (London, Oxford Univ. Press, 1938).

Matthew Arnold, *Culture and Anarchy*, 1869, and *Essays in Criticism*, 1865, First Series. Any edition.

Eneas S. Dallas, *The Gay Science* (London, Chapman and Hall, 1866). 2 vols.

John Stuart Mill, *Autobiography*, 1873 (New York, Columbia Univ. Press, 1924).

John Campbell Shairp, *On Poetic Interpretation of Nature*, 1877 (Boston, Houghton, Mifflin, 1900).

J. B. Selkirk [Brown, James Bucham], *Ethics and Aesthetics of Modern Poetry* (London, Smith, Elder, 1878).

Walter Hamilton, *The Aesthetic Movement in England* (London, 1882).

Francis Palgrave, *Landscape in Poetry from Homer to Tennyson* (London, 1897).

A. E. Housman, *The Name and Nature of Poetry* (New York, Macmillan, 1933).

Delacroix, Eugène, *Journal*, trans. Walter Pach (New York, Covici, Friede, 1937).

The Goncourt Journals, 1851–1870, ed. Lewis Galantière (New York, Doubleday, Doran, 1937).

Some Imagist Poets: An Anthology, Introduction (Boston, Houghton, Mifflin, 1915).

George Moore, Introduction to *An Anthology of Pure Poetry* (New York, Boni and Liveright, 1925).

HISTORICAL AND CRITICAL STUDIES

Babbitt, Irving, *The New Laokoon* (Boston, Houghton, Mifflin, 1910).

Banerjee, Srikumar, *Critical Theories and Poetic Practice in the "Lyrical Ballads"* (London, Williams and Norgate, 1931).

Barstow, Marjorie Latta, *Wordsworth's Theory of Poetic Diction*, ed. A. S. Cook (Yale Studies in English, Vol. LVII; New Haven, Yale Univ. Press, 1917).

Bateson, F. W., *English Poetry and the English Language* (Oxford, Clarendon Press, 1934).

Baudouin, Charles, *Contemporary Studies*, trans. Eden and Cedar Paul (New York, Dutton, 1925).

Beatty, Arthur, *William Wordsworth: His Doctrine and Art in Their Historical Relations* (2d ed.; Univ. of Wisconsin Studies in Language and Literature, No. 24; Madison, 1927).

Belden, Henry Marvin, *Observation and Imagination in Coleridge and Poe,* in *In Honor . . . of Charles Frederick Johnson: Papers, Essays and Stories,* . . . ed. Odell Shepard (Hartford, 1928).

Boas, George, *Philosophy and Poetry* (Norton, Mass., Wheaton College Press, 1932).

Brooks, Cleanth, *Modern Poetry and the Tradition* (Chapel Hill, Univ. of North Carolina Press, 1939).

Burke, Kenneth, *The Philosophy of Literary Form: Studies in Symbolic Action* (Baton Rouge, Louisiana State Univ. Press, 1941).

Chislett, William, Jr., *George Meredith: A Study and an Appraisal* (Boston, Badger, 1925).

Colum, Mary, *From These Roots: The Ideas That Have Made Modern Literature* (New York, Scribner's, 1938).

Damon, S. Foster, *Amy Lowell: A Chronicle* (Boston, Houghton, Mifflin, 1935).

Deane, C. V., *Aspects of Eighteenth Century Nature Poetry* (Oxford, Blackwell, 1935).

Deutsch, Babette, *This Modern Poetry* (New York, Norton, 1935).

De Vane, William Clyde, Jr., *Browning's "Parleyings": The Autobiography of a Mind* (New Haven, Yale Univ. Press, 1927).

———, *A Browning Handbook* (New York, Crofts, 1935).

Dewey, John, *Art as Experience* (New York, Minton, Balch, 1934).

Dobrée, Bonamy, ed. [with Edith C. Batho], *From Anne to Victoria: Essays by Various Hands* (London, Cassell, 1937).

———, *The Victorians and After: 1830–1914* (New York, McBride, 1938).

Durling, Dwight L., *The Georgic Tradition in English Poetry* (Columbia Univ. Studies in English and Comparative Literature, No. 121; Columbia Univ. Press, 1935).

Eastman, Max, *Enjoyment of Poetry, with Other Essays in Aesthetics* (rev. ed.; New York, Scribner's, 1939).

Empson, William, *Seven Types of Ambiguity* (London, Chatto and Windus, 1930).

———, *Some Versions of Pastoral* (London, Chatto and Windus, 1935).

Erhardt-Siebold, E. von, "Harmony of the Senses in English, German, and French Romanticism," *Publ. Mod. Lang. Assoc.,* XLVII (1932), 577–592.

Gingerich, Solomon Francis, *Essays in the Romantic Poets* (New York, Macmillan, 1924).

Grabo, Carl, *The Magic Plant: The Growth of Shelley's Thought* (Chapel Hill, Univ. of North Carolina Press, 1936).

Griggs, Earl Leslie, ed., *Wordsworth and Coleridge: Studies in Honor of George McLean Harper* (Princeton Univ. Press, 1939).

Guérard, Albert, *Art for Art's Sake* (Boston, Lothrop, Lee, and Shepard, 1936).

Hearn, Lafcadio, *Pre-Raphaelite and Other Poets,* ed. John Erskine (New York, Dodd, Mead, 1922).

Hughes, Glenn, *Imagism and the Imagists: A Study in Modern Poetry* (London, Oxford Univ. Press, 1931).

Hulme, T. E., *Speculations: Essays on Humanism and the Philosophy of Art,* ed. Herbert Read (New York, Harcourt, Brace, 1924).

James, D. G., *Scepticism and Poetry: an Essay on the Poetic Imagination* (London, Allen and Unwin, 1937).

Ladd, Henry, *The Victorian Morality of Art* (New York, Long and Smith, 1932).

Leavis, F. R., *Revaluation: Tradition and Development in English Poetry* (London, Chatto and Windus, 1936).

Logan, James V., "Wordsworth and the Pathetic Fallacy," *Mod. Lang. Notes,* LV (1940), 187–191.

————, *The Poetry and Aesthetics of Erasmus Darwin* (Princeton Studies in English, No. 15; Princeton Univ. Press, 1936).

Lowell, Amy, *Six French Poets: Studies in Contemporary Literature* (New York, Macmillan, 1915).

Lowes, John Livingston, *Convention and Revolt in Poetry* (Boston, Houghton, Mifflin, 1919).

Mackail, J. W., *Life of William Morris* (New York, Longmans, Green, 1922). 2 vols. in one.

Mason, Francis C., *A Study in Shelley Criticism* (Mercersburg, Pa., privately printed, 1937).

Mead, George H., *Movements of Thought in the Nineteenth Century,* ed. Merritt H. Moore (Univ. of Chicago Press, 1936).

Miles, Josephine, *Wordsworth and the Vocabulary of Emotion* (Univ. Calif. Publ. English, Vol. 12, No. 1; Berkeley, Univ. of Calif. Press, 1942).

Monk, Samuel H., *The Sublime: A Study of Critical Theories in XVIIIth-Century English* (New York, Modern Language Association of America, 1935).

————, "Anna Seward and the Romantic Poets: A Study in Taste," in *Wordsworth and Coleridge: Studies in Honor of George McLean Harper,* ed. Earl Leslie Griggs (Princeton Univ. Press, 1939).

Nicolson, Harold, *Tennyson* (Boston, Houghton, Mifflin, 1923).

Pierce, Frederick E., *Currents and Eddies in the English Romantic Generation* (New Haven, Yale Univ. Press, 1918).

Pottle, Frederick A., *The Idiom of Poetry* (Ithaca, Cornell Univ. Press, 1941).

Ransom, John Crowe, *The World's Body* (New York, Scribner's, 1938).

Reynolds, Myra, *The Treatment of Nature in English Poetry between Pope and Wordsworth* (2d ed.; Univ. of Chicago Press, 1909).

Richards, I. A., *Coleridge on Imagination* (New York, Harcourt, Brace, 1934).

Ridley, M. R., *Keats' Craftsmanship* (Oxford, Clarendon Press, 1933).

Roberts, Michael, *The Modern Mind* (New York, Macmillan, 1937).

Sackville-West, V., "Some Tendencies of Modern English Poetry," *Essays by Divers Hands,* ed. Margaret L. Woods (Trans. Roy. Soc. Lit., N.S., VII, 39–54; London, Milford, 1927).

Serner, Gunnar, *On the Language of Swinburne's Lyrics and Epics* (Lund, Berlingska Boktryckeriet, 1910).

Sitwell, Edith, *Aspects of Modern Poetry* (London, Duckworth, 1934).

Smith, Arnold, *The Main Tendencies of Victorian Poetry* (Birmingham, St. George Press, 1907).

Smith, Elsie, *An Estimate of Wordsworth by His Contemporaries* (Oxford, Blackwell, 1932).

Snyder, Franklyn Bliss, "Wordsworth's Favorite Words," *Jour. English and Germanic Philol.,* XXII (1923), 253–256.

Sparrow, John, *Sense and Poetry: Essays on the Place of Meaning in Contemporary Verse* (New Haven, Yale Univ. Press, 1934).

Symons, Arthur, *The Romantic Movement in English Poetry* (New York, Dutton, 1909).

————, *The Symbolist Movement in Literature* (rev. ed.; New York, Dutton, 1919).

Tate, Allen, *Reason in Madness: Critical Essays* (New York, Putnam, 1941).

Taube, Edward, "German Influence on English Vocabulary of the Nineteenth Century," *Jour. English and Germanic Philol.,* XXXIX (1940), 486–493.

Trilling, Lionel, *Matthew Arnold* (New York, Norton, 1939).

Vat, Daniel Gerhard van der, *The Fabulous Opera: A Study in the Continuity in French and English Poetry of the Nineteenth Century* (Groningen, Batavia, J. B. Wolter, 1936).

Winters, Yvor, *Primitivism and Decadence: A Study of American Experimental Poetry* (New York, Arrow Editions, 1937).

Winwar [Grebanier], Frances, *Poor Splendid Wings: The Rossettis and Their Circle* (Boston, Little, Brown, 1933).

Zabel, Morton Dauwen, ed., *Literary Opinion in America* (New York, Harpers, 1937).